APPALACHIAN TRIALS

By: Zach Davis

ACKNOWLEDGEMENTS

Although hiking the Appalachian Trail requires a thru-hiker's own legs to walk each of the five million steps from Springer Mountain, Georgia to Mt. Katahdin, Maine, to say that this process can be done alone is nothing short of ficti-tious. Because this book is a non-fiction, I would like to send gratitude to the all of the people who have helped me along the way. During my journey, I received the help and support from countless others. If I were to list out all of the people who offered this assistance, the acknowledgements would be larger than the longest chapter in this book. To the friends and family back home, the trail angels, the readers of my website, the selfless strangers along the trail, and my fellow thru-hikers, *you* are what make the Appala-chian Trail such a truly unique and memorable experience. This book is written in hopes of reciprocating the positive karma that you have shared with me over the course of my half-year on the Appalachian Trail.

I would like to give special thanks to Ian Mangiardi. Without you, this book would not be possible. Not only did you provide me the peace of mind of offering your in depth gear knowledge during any and all hours of the day, your *on-trail* advice is ultimately what allowed me to join this ex-clusive club known as *Appalachian Trail thru-hikers*.

Paula Murphy, having such a creative and passion-ate designer on my side has made the final stages of this process both fun and educational. You are brilliant. Those interested in procuring some high quality design work for themselves need to check out www.branditarians.com.

To B. Hanson Macdonald, your benevolence in offer-ing a complete stranger help in editing an aspiring author's first book is a gift that will not soon be forgotten. Your enthusiasm and diligence for this project is a true reflection of your altruistic and empathetic nature. *Thank you.*

I would like to send a very special thank you to my family. Danielle, your unwavering faith in your brother is what makes an inexperienced camper feel capable of completing a 2,181-mile backpacking voyage. You should probably consider scaling back your confidence before he attempts an even more reckless expedition.

To my father, James, I would like to say thank you for being my *Houston Control* while on the trail. Your boy-scout like research of my *exact* coordinates not only provided an additional layer of comfort in what could have been an unnerving situation, it offered additional peace of mind to the person who needed it most. Which leads me to my next recipient of gratitude.

Michele (aka Mother Badger), *what can I say?* Your anxiety for your son's wellbeing not only drove him into his bravest undertaking to date, it's the foundation for why this book is being written in the first place. And speaking of this book's writing, your tireless and compassionate assistance in the face of a very stubborn and close-minded author played a bigger role in its completion than you can ever know. I take that back. *You do know.*

I love you all dearly.

Table of Contents

"I went to the woods because I wished to live deliberately, to front only the essential facts of life, and see if I could not learn what it had to teach, and not, when I came to die, discover that I had not lived."

- Henry David Thoreau

– INTRODUCTION –

S o you want to thru-hike the Appalachian Trail? You're taking all the steps necessary to prepare yourself. You'll leave no stone unturned. You've reached out to former thru-hikers. You've already picked up other AT prep books. You've spent more time on whiteblaze.net[1] than you can recall. You've lost sleep over whether you should bring a down or synthetic sleeping bag. You've mapped out every location where mail drops will be sent.

And then somehow you stumbled upon *this* book.

"A psychological guide? *To hiking?* Let me guess, one foot in front of the other. Do this approximately 5 million times and you have successfully walked from Springer Mountain, Georgia to Mt. Katahdin, Maine. It's as simple as that, right?"

Right. Except for one thing, *the five million part.*

You might assume that the most difficult aspect of walking the length of the eastern United States would be *purely* physical. Undoubtedly thru-hiking the Appalachian Trail is a physical feat on par with few other challenges in life. You will push your body to new extremes. You will sweat. You will struggle. You will wake up and fall asleep sore. With that said, the physical challenge is *not* why seven in ten aspiring thru-hikers ultimately fall short of their goal.[2]

In no uncertain terms, the psychological and emotional struggle is what drives people off the Appalachian Trail.

It's the unpredictable and daunting psychological impact of your *Appalachian Trials.* It's the homesickness, redundancy, and loneliness. It's the thick, sweltering heat while scaling a shadeless, rock-face mountain. It's trying to sleep through sub-freezing temperatures, hoping that wear-

---

[1] For those who might *not* know, whiteblaze.net is the biggest Appalachian Trail related forum online. I suggest checking it out.

[2] *2,000 Milers.* Retrieved from http://www.appalachiantrail.org/about-the-trail/2000-milers

ing every damn article of clothing in your pack and wrapping your sleeping bag over your head will provide enough warmth to grant a few hours of sleep. It's the constant swarm of mosquitoes, flies, and gnats. It's the boredom that comes from another day of walking through lackluster terrain. It's the pain that strangleholds every muscle of your body upon waking. It's putting on sweat soaked clothes for the fifth morning in a row. It's trying to sleep next to that snoring asshole six inches from your face. It's waking up in a shelter to sound of a mouse eating his way through your backpack. It's pooping in the rain; *have fun trying to wipe.* It's drinking discolored stream water. It's wandering a mile off trail before realizing you have no idea where you are. It's checking your nether regions for parasitic and disease carrying ticks at the end of an exhausting day. It's living in a constant coat of filth. It's walking consecutive days with a set of throbbing blisters between your toes and on the sides of your heals. It's veering off trail to go to the bathroom, only to look down and notice that you're standing in poison ivy. It's rocks eating through your boots and insoles, making it feel as though you're hiking barefoot. It's running through a storm while hearing lighting crash down on every side of you. It's the rustling of an animal prowling outside of your tent just moments before you were *going* to fall asleep. *These are the reasons people throw in the towel, not because a climb is too daunting.*

That's why all the *how-to* advice in the world regarding logistics and terrain, while important, will do nothing to keep you inspired enough to stick with your goal. Going through the hassle of devising an elaborate re-supply schedule -a conventional pre-trail suggestion- gives the illusion of essential preparation, but in reality, 70% of aspiring thru-hikers won't make it to all of their re-supply locations. *If a mail-drop is sent, but no one is there to receive it, does it really exist?* Let's be clear, if finishing the Appalachian Trail is your goal, your time could be better spent.

My time could have been better spent. For the first three months on the trail, I had a total of five mail-drops sent, and that's *only* because conventional AT wisdom suggested that I purchase supplies before leaving. In hindsight, when factoring in the cost of shipping, I didn't save a dime.

Not only did my supply preparation not contribute to my progress on the trail, it was actually counterproductive. I added hassle to my day by having to be at drop-off locations during *their* business hours. As you will soon learn, a life without schedules is one of the true pleasures of the Appalachian Trail.

So who am I to challenge mainstream advice about hiking the AT?

First off, as I'm sure you've already guessed, I am an Appalachian Trail thru-hiker. I accomplished the feat in 2011 in five months and one day. From the months leading up to my hike all the way through my summiting Mt. Katahdin, I kept a running diary on my blog: theGoodBadger.com. I went into the AT as an outsider to the backpacking world; I had literally backpacked zero times before stepping foot onto Springer Mountain.

What was interesting to me about the trail were the mind games, the AT culture, the roller coaster of emotions, and the personal metamorphosis that comes from living in the woods for half a year. On my blog, I detailed not only the struggles within myself, but the larger trends I noticed among my hiking peers. Before I knew it, I was getting more traffic and positive feedback to my website in a single month than I had *in the previous year*. Apparently I had struck a chord.

When I finished the trail, I wanted to find a book detailing the psychological component of hiking the AT to see how it compared to my experiences. What I found baffled me. *This book didn't exist.* There are a plethora of how-to books, none of which deal with the most challenging aspect of the trail?!

Fine, I'll do it.

I wasted no time. I dug through my personal notes, old blog posts, and talked with fellow thru-hikers about their experiences. I wanted to know what separated those who finished from those who failed.

In this process, I found that there are three categories of AT hikers:

1) Those who succumb to the mental challenges and quit
2) Those who rely on sheer determination, grit their teeth, and press onto Katahdin despite being at odds with the process
3) Those who enjoy most, if not all, of their experience while successfully thru-hiking the Appalachian Trail

This book will put you in the third category.

One dirty secret amongst "successful thru-hikers" is that only a fraction of them actually enjoy the *vast majority* of their experience. I'm confident in the years to come, as the Appalachian Trail becomes more popular, we will start collecting more data on hikers' psyches. After all, this is a psychological experiment unlike any other. Without this data, I can only speculate, but I would venture to guess that as many as one in three hikers dislike trail life by the time they reach the latter half of the trail. In reality, Katahdin couldn't come soon enough for them. They finish solely due to persistence.

While their determination is admirable, I don't want you to fall into this second group. It's important to keep in mind that the Appalachian Trail is a half-year unpaid vacation. How determined would you have to be to sit on a beach for the same time span? The trail should be enjoyed, and when joy is difficult to achieve, personal growth should become the focus.

Still, you might be skeptical. Perhaps you're thinking, "People who would love a half-year backpacking trip possess a rare and inherent quality; they're wired differently. It's built into their DNA, and I just wasn't bestowed with those attributes."

I understand why you might feel this way, but allow me to explain why you're wrong. *I* successfully thru-hiked the Appalachian Trail, and genuinely enjoyed the experience.

In theory, there was no one more ill-prepared to thru-hike the Appalachian Trail than me. I'm a computer guy, not a camping guy. I owned *none* of the gear necessary for a half-year backpacking trip. I had never set up a tent or built a campfire. The *only* thing I had going for me was that I was in decent shape and good health. But as you will learn in Chapter 5, even that was taken away from me. Now that I've completed this task, I look back at my experience with only fond memories, even when sober.

The bottom line is this: not only can you achieve your goal of hiking from Georgia to Maine, you *can, and should,* enjoy the process. This book will show you how.

Since you picked up this book, *I feel responsible for your success.* Your summiting Mt. Katahdin and enjoying the process sincerely matters to me. I'm convinced the rest of the book will help you accomplish just that.

But there is another reason you should read *Appalachian Trials.* You're not the only one who will be presented with psychological hurdles. Family and friends who are clueless about your upcoming adventure may be anxious as well. And trust me on this one, calming their fears benefits you. They'll get off your back. They'll join your team. They'll applaud your seemingly *idiotic* journey instead of questioning it. Because after all, knowledge assuages fear. So when you're done reading this book, pass it on to the anxiety-ridden people in your life. Better yet, tell them to get their own copy.

Here's another reason reading this book should be on your short list of things to do before leaving for the trail. Perhaps you're someone who isn't yet convinced traversing the world's oldest mountain range is something you want to do. The fact that you're reading this book tells me that you're sufficiently curious about it. With a little nudge, you might just decide to leave behind the comforts of home and embark on this journey of a lifetime. At the very least, you'll get a sneak peak into the psyche of a thru-hiker. Knowing what's in a thru-hiker's pack is nice. But if *finishing* is your concern, knowing what's inside a thru-hiker's *mind* is what matters.

I'm convinced that for every person who actually embarks on the AT, there are countless others who talk themselves out of it for one reason or another. Don't be one of those people. Not only will I provide that friendly nudge to pack your pack, I'll be with you every step along the way.

This book is divided into four sections. The first three- pre-trail, on-trail, and *(you guessed it)* post-trail- will both prepare you against the common pitfalls aspiring thru-hikers fall into, as well as provide you the tools necessary to keep a strong mindset when you're confronted with your own *Appalachian trials*. The fourth section is a collection of *bonus* material including a detailed gear chapter, how to avoid the AT's greatest and most downplayed risk, and a thorough FAQ, including how to save money before and during your thru-hike.

One final note- throughout *Appalachian Trials*, there is an emphasis on the challenges associated with thru-hiking the Appalachian Trail. My objective with this book is to prepare you for the obstacles that you can expect to encounter during a half-year in the woods. The *only* way I can properly accomplish this is by shining a light on these darker regions.

For this reason, however, it could be interpreted that I have a negative perspective of the AT. In reality, nothing could be further from the truth. My thru-hike was the best five months and one day of my life to date. That said, a large reason I was able to not only finish the trail, but sincerely enjoy it, was due to my honest and open confrontation of the obstacles ahead. This book will require you to do the same.

So whether you're already planning your journey into the woods or you're still straddling the fence, join me in Chapter 1, where you will glimpse my pre-hike self, convincing you evermore that if *I* was able to triumph over my *Appalachian trials*, you too will prevail over yours.

SECTION ONE:
PRE-TRAIL

Chapter 1 Computer Nerd Turned Bear Grylls

*I*t *was early November.* I had mentally committed to the insane: next spring I would backpack from Georgia to Maine. It was almost too ridiculous to comprehend. In a state of excitement/bewilderment I called one of my former roommates and good friend, Mitch.

Me: Guess what?
Mitch: What?
Me: I'm going to hike the Appalachian Trail...
Mitch: (Without hesitation) Pshht. *No you're not.*
Me: Wait....what? You don't even know what it is. How can you be so dismissive?
Mitch: My sister's boyfriend is a former thru-hiker. They live in a town right on the trail. I know plenty about the AT, and there's no way you're going to hike the whole thing.

There are two takeaways from the above conversation.

1) From someone who knew me well, the honest assessment of my chances to successfully complete a 2,181-mile backpacking trip clearly pointed toward failure.
2) I need new friends.

At the time of this conversation, I had slept in a tent a total of two nights during my 25 years on earth – once on a *car camping* trip, once in a friend's backyard. As previously mentioned, I had set up a tent zero times, which matched my experience in building fires or fastening a fully-loaded backpack. My total outdoors practice consisted of drinking beer near a campfire (which I'm quite good at), pretending I could accurately reproduce animal mating calls (I can't) and scorching marshmallows (I sorely lack patience). A friend once said that if pressed to list my "Top Skills Essential for Survival in Nature", my "affinity for bandanas" would rank #1, which, as it turns out, is not even a skill.

In other words, although Mitch's response lacked tact, his assessment was fair.

So why would someone who had never been back-packing in his entire life want to take part in a cross-country backpacking trip?

In a word: *dissatisfaction.*

Backtrack to October of the same year.

At the time, I was self-employed, doing Internet marketing and consulting for small businesses. There's a perception that self-employment is the ultimate freedom. If done correctly, this can be true. In my situation, however, my *so-called freedom* translated to 70+ hours in front of my laptop each week. There was *always* something to be done. Because I didn't impose any sort of schedule upon myself, my default activity was work. Even when I did take a break from work- my form of escape was to browse Facebook, Twitter, write for my website, or watch Netflix. *I was under the spell of the screen.*

Although I could sense that my lifestyle was unsatis-fying and unhealthy, both physically and mentally, I was locked into a routine. The first thing I would do in the morning was roll over, open my laptop and check my e-mail. This was entirely unconscious. When I managed to pull myself away from the screen to go to the gym, for a hike or a run, I would instantly feel better. Unfortunately those times were few and far between, and I'd be back in front of the screen before I knew it.

On one of the rare evenings where I decided to partake in social activity, I joined my friend, John, at the local watering hole. Everyone has *that friend* who is constantly organizing his/her next musical festival, vacation, party, and so on. John is my version of this friend. We were a few beers deep and he was updating me with the latest edition of his upcoming journeys.

"...and I know you'll like *this one*," John paused. His eyes grew wide. I knew something off the wall was to follow. *"So there's this trail...."*

John proceeded to inform me of his plans to thru-hike the Appalachian Trail- a 2,181-mile trip through the oldest mountain range in the United States[3]! John had more camping experience than me, but not by a lot. To say that he was an experienced outdoorsman was a vast over-statement. At the time, John was working an IT job for a major golf equipment company. Much like myself, his competencies were behind a computer screen, not in the woods.

My stomach turned, I could feel an alarming energy overcome my body. The idea was insane, but on some level I knew this was the "out" I needed to catapult me from my unsatisfying routine.

"That's amazing. *I'm coming with you.*"

And so it was set. Without having any idea what I was getting myself into, I had just verbally committed to the biggest adventure of my life.

Fast forward to January

It was officially less than three months from my departure for the trail. My obsessive work ethic was dying, or more accurately put, was being funneled into researching the trail. Websites such as whiteblaze.net offered an ocean of information. It was helpful, but the quantity of advice was overwhelming, plus, opinions were often contradictory. I

---

[3] And world.

had specific questions (since I knew *nothing*, I had *a lot* of them) and was having trouble getting the right answers.

In a rare moment of social media fate, I was put in touch with Josh Turner of Camping Gear TV (Camping-GearTV.com). Not only did Josh put me in contact with many of the sponsors of his show, which ultimately led to gear donations for John and me, but he connected me with Ian Mangiardi. Ian is a former AT thru-hiker and co-founder of The Dusty Camel (TheDustyCamel.org), a website offering backpacking gear reviews. In no uncertain terms, Ian became my AT therapist/coach from that point until my departure for the trail.

In the process of talking me off the ledge several times as a result of severe pre-trail anxiety, Ian helped me to prepare mentally for what might occur over the next half year. More importantly Ian gave me tips on *how to approach* these challenging times. Up until this point, I was having trouble finding information regarding the psychological battles one would confront along the trail. His forthrightness was a breath a fresh air.

I was beginning to realize that if I had any shot of completing the AT, I needed to prepare myself mentally. Instead of ignoring the obstacles ahead, I had to confront them. More accurately, I had to confront myself. I accepted that the AT was not only a geographical journey, but a personal one as well.

Although I eventually revised Ian's advice to incorporate what I already knew about human psychology and self-help, his words marked a sea change in my approach.

Instead of going on trial-run camping trips or spending hours deliberating about the perfect gear, I used my remaining time to focus on the gear between my ears. I predicted that building my mental muscle would build the endurance necessary for success.

My prediction proved correct.

Fast forward to April (On the trail for one month)

I had just returned from an unforeseen trip to Silicon Valley for a job interview with the only company on earth capable of enticing me off the trail (I'll elaborate in Chapter 6). By this point, the rest of my group was already one hundred miles ahead. I was now hiking the Appalachian Trail *on my own*. Although I was a tad nervous about confronting the woods alone, I quickly proved to myself that this concern was unnecessary.

I was stealth camping in remote areas off the trail, building my own campfires, setting up my own bear-bags, and reaching a new height of affinity for my surroundings. I would go a full 48 hours before encountering another human being. Not only did I survive, I thrived. In just one month's time, I was a new person. At the very least, I was the same person with a radically new skill set. *I had complete confidence in myself.*

And in the five months that it took me to complete the trail, I would spend more time by myself than in the company of others. I would have experiences that will vividly live in my mind until the day I die.

Without significant pre-trail preparation, it's safe to assume that I would have fallen into the unfortunate majority of hikers who drop off the trail. Wandering into the dark woods in the middle of nowhere by myself would have been enough for me to hit the panic button. As it turned out, I wasn't fazed in the least.

Instead, I would go on to tackle obstacles far greater than I ever would have predicted. Not once did I consider getting off the trail. Instead, I would spend most (although, not all) of my days smiling unconditionally. I attribute this entirely to the work I did on myself before ever leaving home.

So now you must be thinking, "Okay, great, so what *is* your advice? How can *I* mentally prepare myself?" Great question, that's the subject of our next chapter.

CHAPTER 2 MENTALLY PREPARING

W hy prepare mentally for "a hike"?
There are a lot of situations in life that require mental preparation- public speaking, a first date, attempting to lose a substantial amount of weight. *But a hike*? Really?

Really.

You've probably been on hikes before. Maybe you've backpacked. Perhaps you've even been on *extended* backpacking trips. You know what to expect. You wake up in your tent/shelter, eat, walk, poop, walk, eat, walk, eat, walk, poop, eat, set up camp, sleep, rinse and repeat. You didn't do any mental preparation and made it out just fine.

Non-competitive outdoor activities shouldn't require mental preparation. Such activities are typically done for the leisure's sake. Backpacking is no exception. So why am I suggesting you do something that, at least on the surface, doesn't seem entirely necessary?

You know what you're giving up with your new lifestyle: a warm bed, a diet consisting of *real food*, regular access to a shower, electronic entertainment on demand, instant communication with friends, family, and co-workers and so on. You wouldn't even consider hiking the Appalachian Trail if you hadn't come to grips with this. In fact, you're probably *excited* to do your best Thoreau impression and take part in a simpler, Walden-like lifestyle. *Minimally, you're not all that concerned about the lifestyle change.*

And for the first few weeks or so, you may question why I insisted that you prepare at all. After all, early on your hike will seem relatively effortless, at least from a psychological standpoint. The endorphins that accompany the increased heart rate offer a hiker's high for the bulk of the day. The breath-taking beauty of mountain summit views and the escape from a rigid daily schedule will undoubtedly feel like a net lifestyle gain. But take note, the excitement will eventually fade, and when it does, you better be prepared.

For this reason, it's not the first month that you need to prepare for; *it's months two through seven we're concerned with.*

In the beginning of your hike everything will be exhilarating, even the hard times. Your first scamper through a hailstorm, the first time you wander off course, the first rattlesnake you narrowly avoid step on- situations that might arouse fear and or frustration- leave you feeling on top of the world at the event's conclusion. There's a feeling of invincibility associated with overcoming these natural obstacles.

But, eventually aggravation replaces exhilaration (I will expand upon this later). While running through a lightning storm may have been a rush in the beginning, eventually your mind starts to say, "I'm wet. My tent is wet. I'm hungry, but if I stop to eat here, my food will get wet and I will get cold. I could be watching this storm from the comforts of my couch while watching a *"Where Are They Now?"* marathon. *Why am I doing this again?"*

This is a profound and *extremely* important question.

Why *are* you doing this, again?

Because you *will* undoubtedly ask yourself this question, it's important to confront this *now*, so you have a compelling answer to give yourself when, not if, this occurs.

You might be hesitant to simply take my word for it now, but please, take this seriously. It's not coincidence that seventy per cent of attempting thru-hikers don't make it to Katahdin. I met former military and highly experienced backpackers who would eventually throw in the towel. They weren't in over their heads. Their "*skill set*" was likely far ahead of yours. Certainly it was light years ahead of mine. Even from a mental fortitude standpoint, someone who's gone through the rigors of basic training can withstand a great deal of turmoil. They've gone through months, if not years, of grueling exercises and simulations to keep their mindset strong when shit hits the fan. So, how is it that someone of their ilk could cave in during what essentially amounts to a half-year vacation?

Because when it comes to backpacking 2,220 miles, the greatest determining factor of success is purpose.

In the throes of battle, (e.g. your third consecutive day of hiking through a rainstorm), it becomes much easier to forget *your* purpose. You'll remind yourself that hiking the AT is a voluntary practice. No one has a gun to your head. You're willingly walking through the rain. To most, that's *insanity*. Right now, sitting on the couch, reading this book, the idea might seem fun. When the inside of your boots have collected a small puddle, it might not seem quite so fun. There will come a day, when you ask yourself this all too important question. *Why am I doing this again?*

I was sure this day would come. *It did.* Instead of being at the mercy of my emotions when it did, I needed a plan. I fully invested my emotions into building a compelling answer to this question before ever leaving for the trail. Zach needed to convince *Badger[4]* why he was doing what he was doing.

So- I made lists.

"If you don't know where you are going, you might wind up someplace else." -
Yogi Berra

The first list, entitled *"I am Thru-Hiking the Appalachian Trail because..."* focused solely on the *why*. This and all of the subsequent titles were positively stated to reinforce my conviction in finishing.

---

[4] What would go onto become my *trail name*.

Here are some of the examples from my list:

I am Thru- Hiking the Appalachian Trail because...

- I need some time to re-evaluate the direction of my career
- I am craving an adventure larger than life
- Life is short, do awesome shit, stupid
- Postponing happiness until retirement is a flawed life approach
- I have the rest of my life to sit in front of a computer
- I want to expose myself to a new environment
- I need a change of pace
- What I'm currently doing *isn't working*
- I suck at backpacking

The second list, entitled *"When I Successfully Thru-Hike the Appalachian Trail, I will..."*, focused on the personal benefits I helped to acquire from thru-hiking the trail. I imagined a set of rewards waiting for me atop Katahdin, like presents sitting under a Christmas tree. Although it's silly, it got me where I wanted to go. Additionally, I can say with conviction that each of these "presents" are now in my possession. They are:

When I successfully thru-hike the Appalachian Trail, I will...

- have an unshakeable confidence
- have the story of a lifetime
- restore a clearer sense of presence
- turn a glaring weakness into a strength
- see life in a new light
- have overcome the greatest challenge of my life
- be a better listener
- leverage this accomplishment to create new momentum
- have a clearer idea of what I want to do in life

I don't think I'm going out on the limb by saying that you have your own compelling reasons for hiking the AT. Maybe you're unsatisfied with the current direction that your life is heading. Maybe you're seeking a change of pace or a new challenge. Maybe you're an adventure junkie and the AT is your crown jewel. Perhaps thru-hiking the Appalachian Trail is something you've wanted to do for *many* years, but haven't had the time and/or money to take it on, and now you do. Whatever the reason, take some time to consider *why* you're *really* doing this. Remember, there will come a time when you will ask yourself this very question. Show me someone without a compelling answer and I'll show you someone who will eventually be homebound.

Take *at least* twenty minutes to consider all of the reasons you want to hike the Appalachian Trail. Include as many benefits as possible that you anticipate getting out of hiking the trail. Be honest with yourself. The AT is unique opportunity for growth. Failing to take advantage of this is a mistake. What sorts of changes would you like to see in your life?

I've included a series of template lists for you to use in the appendices of this book. If you'd rather not rip pages out of this book, or are working on an e-reader, I've also made print-out .pdf versions available on my website at the following address: **http://zrdavis.com/why-hike**

Commit your responses to writing. *Do it now.*
...
Seriously. Do it.
...
I'm not kidding.
...
Now.
...
I'll wait.
...
(.....humming Ace of Base songs....)
...
(*"Allllll that she wants...."*)
...
Ok, you did it?

...
Good.

Your list will be a powerful tool to keep you motivated during your *Appalachian trials*. However, focusing on the positive traits that you'll acquire upon finishing is only half the battle. You also need to create a list of *negative* consequences associated with *quitting* on the trail.

This list is titled *"If I give up on the Appalachian Trail, I will..."* The following are some examples from my list.

If I give up on the Appalachian Trail, I will...

- never believe in myself
- not like the person I see in the mirror
- continue to settle in all other aspects of my life (career-wise, physically, relationships, etc.)
- not be the person I believe that I am
- carry the baggage of shame
- reveal my lack of confidence in my posture
- not be able to attract others

Again, take *at least* twenty minutes to consider all the potential consequences of giving up on your goal. Really put yourself into the mental/emotional state of how you'll feel if you don't follow through. How will you cope with this? Will you start eating/drinking more? Will you slack off in your career? What other areas of your life will you start compromising? How will you treat those around you? What effect will that have on your relationships? What will your skeptics think of you? *Go deep.*

Write down everything you feel. Err on the side of being too descriptive and/or redundant rather than being brief.

Bring these lists with you. Every time you sense yourself starting to slip emotionally, pull out and review your lists. Better yet, don't let yourself get to that point. Remind yourself as often as possible. Every two weeks, every week, every day. The work you do with this before you leave for the trail may very well be the difference between Katahdin and quitting. At the very least, it will help to boost your spirits, even if you aren't to the point where you're contemplating vacating the trail.

I reviewed my list once a week or so prior to passing out. Not only did this help in keeping me determined, but it served as a reminder of what I was originally looking to get from the trip. You have plenty of free time on the trail. You'll never have a better opportunity to clear your head and re-install new software, or at least clean out the viruses.

The above lists are only the first step in your pre-trail work. Now, let's step it up a notch.

This following step is *crazy* important. I'm talking Gary Busey crazy.

Publicly state your mission.

You're about to embark on something truly epic, now is no time to be bashful. You are going to *walk* from Georgia to Maine. Let people know! Tell friends. Tell family. Tell co-workers. Tell neighbors. Tell the barista at Starbucks. Tell your mailman. Tell your hair stylist/barber. Tell your pets. Tell Facebook. Tell Twitter. Tell YouTube. Do you have a website? Yes? Announce it there. No? Step 1) start one. Step 2) TELL PEOPLE!

Publicly announcing your thru-hike is crucial for two reasons. First, it makes your plan more real. Seeing the reactions in others will help to put into perspective how *badass* you really are! Secondly, and more importantly, it makes you accountable. More accurately, others will hold you accountable. If you want to back out of the trail at any point, not only do you have to look yourself in the mirror, but you'll have a lot of people to answer to. Oftentimes, the shame associated with coming back home with your tail between your legs will be enough motivation to keep you going. You want to use this social pressure in your favor.

This tactic helped me immensely. When I announced to my family that I was going to thru-hike the Appalachian Trail, they only took me half seriously. They knew that I wasn't exactly the *outdoorsy* type. Time and again, I would bring up the fact that I was going to hike this 2,200 mile trail, but I could see eyes were glazing over. It wasn't until I wrote a post announcing my plans to thru-hike on the Good Badger (theGoodBadger.com) that they took me seriously. They knew more than anyone else how much I value my site and its readers. Although they thought maybe I was just blowing smoke up the collective family butt, there was no way I would bullshit my readers. It was at that exact moment where my mom's anxiety level escalated into red, and would hover near the *panic zone* until the day I would summit Katahdin.

Additionally, all of my friends knew about this. I had a going away party in both San Diego and Chicago[5]. I couldn't imagine coming back and looking these people in the eyes saying, "Yeah, well I tried, but it was *really* hard. I'm sure you understand." Having to explain my failure seemed far more difficult than walking.

In retrospect, I'm very happy that publicly announced my intent to thru-hike. You will be too, *trust me*.

Wanna make a bet?

In the process of telling people that you're going on a 2,200-mile hike, you will likely encounter a few skeptics along the way. As you might have guessed, I had more than my fair share. Although it may seem like an attempt to shake your confidence, their skepticism can be a powerful tool to further motivate yourself.

Instead of getting defensive, or questioning yourself, test *their* confidence. Find out exactly *how sure* they are of your failure by asking them to put their money where their *nay-saying* mouth is. Remind them that only one in four attempting thru-hikers end up finishing (you know, to get a better payout).

Not only is betting on yourself a powerful tactic for motivation, it also takes advantage of a trait ingrained in all humans: aversion to loss. We hate losing. We hate losing

---

5 And by "party", I mean drinking with friends and them telling me that I was as good as dead.

even more than we *love* winning[6]. By making some sort of monetary wager on your success, the loss associated with not finishing will be more tangible and motivating.

Acceptance

Your final step in your mental preparation is an important one: *acceptance.*

If your pre-hike emotional state is any anything like mine was, you might be a tad on the anxious side[7]. Instead of trying to fight these feelings, allow them to occur freely, and more importantly, don't let them dissuade you from the trail. Not only is this perfectly normal, it's healthy. Nervous energy is a common precursor to positive change. You've probably already experienced similar emotions during another transitional phase in your life, whether it be going away to college, moving to a new city, taking a new job or changing career paths and so on. I'm guessing the change was necessary to your life, and ultimately had a positive outcome. The trail is no different. You have good reasons for hiking the Appalachian Trail. If you don't believe me, consult your lists

It might be helpful to write your pre-trail feelings down. For starters, it's therapeutic. Putting your emotions into words will help to diffuse any negative energy. Also, once you have successfully completed the trail, your writing will provide a powerful barometer allowing you to see how far you've come. It will help you gauge how much you have grown as a person.

---

6 Gächter S., Johnson, Eric J., Herrmann A., (2010, November 16). Individual-level loss aversion in riskless and risky choices. Retrieved from: http://cess.nyu.edu/schotter/wp-content/uploads/2010/02/%E2%80%9CUnderstanding-Overbidding-Using-the-Neural-Circuitry-of-Reward-to-Design-Economic-Auctions%E2%80%9D.pdf

7 *Understatement of the millennium.* I'm pretty sure I slept for a total of 85 minutes *total* in the final month leading up to the trail. I could've easily fit all of my gear in the bags under my eyes.

Summary

By following through with the above steps, you will be light-years ahead of others in your quest to successfully thru-hike the AT. More importantly, you will be prepared when you come to your first set of *Appalachian trials*. And I have a good guess precisely *where* that will happen. But before we get to that, let's look at what you can expect at *the beginning* of the trail.

SECTION TWO:
ON-TRAIL

CHAPTER 3 THE BEGINNING

Y ou've finally done it. All your hard work prior to leaving has led up to this moment; you're stepping foot onto Springer Mountain (once you complete the grueling hike up Amicalola Falls, that is)[8].
You're at the beginning. You realize there's a great deal ahead of you, but at last you are finally chipping away at that daunting 2,200-mile total.

The question now becomes, what happens to your mental state once on the trail? If there is one thing you need to know about these early stages of the trail, it's that you're stepping foot onto.....

The Appalachian Roller Coaster

Hydroplaning Into Hiawassee

It was night number five for Whoop[9] and Badger. We were camped out next to the shelter at Tray Mountain. The evening's temperature was 25 degrees warmer than the previous night, which touched down to 23°F. This warm front was two things: one, a welcome relief from the sub-freezing temperatures of the night before and two, the catalyst to a

---

[8] There is an alternate route to a trailhead one mile north of Springer Mountain. Hikers fortunate enough to have someone to drive them to this waypoint must then backtrack a mile to Springer Mountain. This is the route that Whoop and Badger took. For exact directions to this trailhead visit: www.zrdavis.com/SpringerAlt

[9] John's trail name.

ball-busting thunderstorm beginning the following morning. To this point, we had yet to see any rain. That day, however, we were in store for a frigid, windy, downpour.

We quickly and haphazardly threw our gear into our packs for the quick eleven-mile scamper toward Dick's Creek Gap, where we could then catch a hitch into Hiawasee. Because the previous days' hikes were both a few miles longer than what was in front of us, we had agreed that today would seem like a day off. We were way off.

For those who have never scurried double-digit miles through a lightning storm, you can't fully empathize with how distressing this is (you soon will). Each explosion of thunder causes your heart to jump into the back of your throat, only to quickly drop back down into the depths of your anus. The day's terrain included the most challenging ascents and descents we had experienced on the trail thus far. Typically the ascents are the part of the trail a hiker dreads most. On this day, however, the increased workload from these inclines was the only way to generate any body heat. Because one misstep would result in picking myself out of a mud puddle, my neck remained locked in the downward position to ensure a strategic placement of each step throughout the hike. And when I say *hike*, I mean it only in the loosest sense of the word. This particular activity is more accurately described as controlled hydroplaning.

Once we reached Dick's Creep Gap, we still had another hurdle to jump. Hiawassee is ten miles to the east, and neither of us had cell service to call for a shuttle to come pick our miserable asses up. To make matters worse, another group of hikers who had just come from Hiawassee wasted no time in telling us that, "Every room in town was booked." We agreed to give it a shot anyway. Within a few minutes, a friendly southern gentleman (the south really does breed the kindest people on earth), gave us a ride to the Hiawassee Inn.

At this point, Whoop and I were at each other's throats. We attacked everything the other person said, for no other reason than we were both stressed out and didn't know how to handle it like civilized creatures. In our defense, creatures of the woods lack civility.

When we got to the Inn, the guy behind the desk, Dale, quickly informed us that he didn't have any rooms available for the night. Although this news was not what we wanted to hear, he let us stand under the lobby's heater and change into dry clothes; our short-term needs were met. And I don't mean this in the, "I need coffee in the morning," sense. You *want* coffee in the morning. We *needed* to dry off before our bodies went into hypothermic shock. Upon removing our gloves and socks, he and I compared our hands and feet. Both of us were prunes. We had lost all color except for a few sporadic blue spots. Our extremities looked like blueberries in yogurt. We laughed only because crying was the other alternative. *There's no crying in hiking.*

Dale allowed us to use the inn's Internet so we could find other accommodations. We called everywhere in town. The responses confirmed what the hiker at Dick's Creek Gap had already told us- no vacancy. Finally, we called the Ramada on the opposite side of town. "Yes sir, we have two rooms left for the night. Would you like to secure one now?" Without inquiring about price, I immediately responded, "Yeah, yes, ya we'll take it. *Yes.*"

As we walked into our luxury hotel room (yeah, we overpaid a bit; we deserved it), we both finally got a chance to decompress. We dumped our muddy stuff all over the bathroom[10], and I deferred to Whoop who requested the first shower. What felt like a half hour later (because it was), he walked out and said, "Dude, the shower head....". *That's all he said.*

The wait was worth it (not that I had any choice). He was right. *The showerhead....* It had eight different settings, none of which were freezing rain and lightning. As I toggled between each one, it was nothing shy of bliss and easily the most appreciated shower of my life. As chance would have it, it also happened to be thirty minutes in duration. Apparently that's how long it takes to rinse misery from off of a human body.

Because eating in the freezing rain requires standing still, we both passed on consuming any food throughout the

---

[10] Be courteous when in town; do as I say, not as I do.

day. Needless to say, we were pretty famished at this point. We called a shuttle service aptly named, "Gene Shuttles" to see how much a ride to the nearest all-you-can-eat pizza buffet (a thru-hiker staple) would cost. Gene answered his cell phone:

Gene: "Hello."
Badger: Stunned by the informal greeting, "Uh, ya, hi, is this the shuttle service?"
Gene: "Oh, ya. I can shuttle."
Badger: Slightly confused, "Cool. How much would it be for a ride to Big Al's Pizza?"
Gene: "Pizza huh? I could go for some pizza. Don't worry about it, what time do you want me to pick you up?"
Badger: "In 30 minutes?"
Gene: "See you then."

It turns out Gene Shuttles wasn't a professional shuttle service, it was just *Gene*, a super awesome retired guy. He picks up side jobs, not because he needs the money, but because he's looking to keep busy. He took us out for an all you-can-eat-pizza buffet that I will not soon forget, gave us a brief tour of the Hiawassee, and gave us a ride to the grocery store so we could stock up on beer (*too much beer*) - all free of charge.

In the span of only a few hours, we had gone from agony to ecstasy. *Before*, we were worried about one hundred million volts of electricity coursing through our veins, we were freezing, we were hungry, we were uncertain of where we were going to sleep that night, we hated one another; our spirits were dogshit.

And *now*, we were warm, comfortable, full, and had eight different pressure combinations in our showerhead. We were on top of the world. We were drunk. We were friends again. We had made our first official run on the Appalachian Roller Coaster.

Enjoy the ride.

So what can you takeaway from the above story?

The AT has lows

It won't take too much time on trail before you learn that you are at the mercy of Mother Nature. She will have her way with you. You will wake up to the sound of thunder rumbling in the distance. Before you know it, that distance has closed, and you are in the heart of the storm. You hurriedly scramble to get your life together and rush toward your intended destination. But there's no escaping the reality in front of you. You're six miles from the next shelter, but the heart of the storm is sitting overhead. Before long, you come to learn that your rain gear doesn't prevent moisture from getting in, it merely slows it down. Your hands and feet are shriveled, colorless, and raw. Your boots have collected a small puddle on the inside. Your already increased heart rate is elevated even higher with each explosion of thunder. You're on high alert. You haven't blinked in over an hour, much less taken time for a break.

The AT has highs

Eventually, however, Mother Nature will come around. The clouds will clear, the sun will appear, and she will smile upon you.

Regardless of the elements, you will eventually find some respite from the chaos. You'll reach that shelter, only to find other hikers who have just fought the same battle. You and your fellow sheltermates will commiserate over what you have just gone through. A unique and strong community builds. Someone in the group will offer up their cigarette, spliff, or whiskey flask. Your nerves will settle and all that remains will be residue adrenaline. You will be left with a sense of invincibility. You'll have proven to yourself that, although the elements may be challenging, it's a challenge that you can overcome.

Or maybe you'll get to town. You'll discover the real contrast to life on the Appalachian Trail, a life in which doesn't live exclusively *on* the trail. You'll get to that all you-can-eat buffet. You'll down a few beers. You'll grab a warm shower. Doing your laundry will seem like a reward rather than a chore. You'll meet the kind souls who surround the trail; the trail angels who dedicate their free time to providing you and your fellow hikers some much appreciated magic[11].

There is a saying on the trail, "Don't decide to quit on a rainy day, don't decide to quit on an uphill." This embodies the roller coaster perfectly. Just when you think things are at their worst, serendipity will strike, and your day will turn around. In short, the Appalachian Trail is a lesson in volatility. Like riding a roller coaster, the motions are out of your control. Your only job is to enjoy the ride.

Some context

To clarify- not every day during this initial stretch will be a roller coaster. Some days, will just be normal, peaceful days.

The point is that in relation to the rest of the trail, this initial period will be much more of a roller coaster. The remainder of the trail stabilizes not because the intensity of external events lets up, but because you eventually adapt. For this reason, the ups and downs will have a much more profound effect on you early on.

And because the period is such a roller coaster ride, it is my opinion this initial stage is actually *easier* than the rest of the trail. Although, over time, you will be better equipped to handle these various lows – the lightning storms, wandering off trail, misjudging and consequently rationing your food supply – the rush of adrenaline associated with overcoming these obstacles will be replaced by irritation. The challenges will be hard, but they'll be temporarily exciting. However, this won't always be the case.

So what will the beginning of the trail be like for you?

All that I can say with confidence is that the pendulum swing is more extreme. You're not yet used to the Appala-

---

[11] If you're interested in learning more about Appalachian Trail magic, I've written an extensive post on this subject: http://zrdavis.com/trailmagic

chian Roller Coaster. Every day is an adventure. Even if it's difficult, it's thrilling. If you can't get up for that, the Appalachian Trail probably isn't for you.

Also, keep in mind that these early hills and valleys are where you develop a sense of appreciation. This is a huge part of the trail. A frigid rainstorm is what makes a warm shower a life altering experience. An eleven-mile hydroplane hike while not eating is what makes a pizza buffet feel like a miracle straight from God's oven. The constant fear of getting struck by lighting is what makes the buzz that follows a few beers the equivalent to bliss. Exposing yourself to these elements is what makes the refuge that follows so enjoyable. A deprivation lifestyle gives us the opportunity to fully appreciate *what we do have*. This is what the Appalachian Trail is all about.

Why People Drop Out Early

I'm aware that the dropout rate is relatively high in this initial stretch of the trail. I remember coming across a gentleman in his early forties who was sprawled across the trail and vomiting profusely. This was less than eighteen miles from Springer Mountain. I'm guessing he didn't make it to Katahdin.

Another hiker I met on the first day, Mick Jagger, told me that he had decided to thru-hike a couple of weeks before leaving. His pack weighed over sixty pounds. He was wearing jeans. I'm guessing he probably didn't make it either (although I *hope* he did, Mick Jagger was awesome).

So how can I make the claim that the Appalachian Trail is actually easier in these early stages if so many people drop out? In my opinion, there are two primary reasons why people drop out in these early phases.

1) People push themselves past their limits.

Although coming onto the trail in great shape will certainly help tremendously, it is by no means is a prerequisite. You can go onto the Appalachian Trail at pretty much any level of fitness[12]. You can consider the first three to five weeks of the trail your training for the rest of your hike. That said, your shape should dictate your initial level of output. If you go on the trail as someone who competes in an Ironman for fun, you probably don't have to pace yourself all that much. If you go on the trail as a sedentary, overweight couch potato, you need to be extra cautious. Most people will fall somewhere between these two categories.

The best piece of advice I can offer for this initial stretch is to cover less ground than you feel you're capable of. This beginning stage is the point where you're the most injury-prone. Unless you've done a lot of sport-specific training before hitting the trail, there's no way you can, nor should, hit the ground running. Your muscles, and more importantly, joints, will take a serious beating. Your body will go into shock. You will wake up sore everyday, and without rest, the pain begins to accumulate. There is no way around this. I didn't talk to a single person in the beginning who didn't complain of stiff joints and sore muscles. That's what happens when you strap thirty pounds to your back and climb mountains for consecutive weeks. No surprise there.

Advil is an extremely common substance on the AT for this reason. I saw some people taking up to six to eight pills per day. Because ibuprofen (referred to as "Vitamin I" on the trail) is an anti-inflammatory, it will reduce swelling, thus making your hike more bearable, especially in the morning[13]. However, never take any medication, prescribed or over-the-counter, to mask pain in order to continue hiking. Pain is your body's way of telling you that something is wrong. Ignoring this signal is a one-way ticket to Injuryville (population: you). Keep this in mind.

Those are the physical reasons for not pushing yourself excessively in the beginning. From a psychological

---

[12] To be clear, I don't recommend going into the trail in poor shape. If you're not in great shape, you *can* still successfully thru-hike, you will just have more going against you. Being in good shape leading up to the trail will serve to ease your transition, thus making it far less likely for you to get frustrated and drop out.

[13] The actual act of walking seems to reduce early morning pain. Within a couple hours of hiking, stiffness and soreness will decrease.

standpoint, you will need to develop a marathon mentality (covered in chapter 8) if you plan on succeeding. Pushing yourself to the limit in these early stages, even if you are able to stave off injury, will prove to be a dangerous approach in regards to your sanity. Maine is a long ways off. A long, long, long ways off. Cool your jets, friend. You'll get there. Be patient.

As a general precaution, treat the first three weeks of your thru-hike as your adaptation period. If you're in poor shape, start with six to ten miles a day. If you're in good shape, start with ten to sixteen miles per day. If this proves to be relatively easy after a few days, start to slowly increase your mileage. There's no penalty for doing too few miles. The punishment for hiking too many, however, is steep. If your body starts to exhibit signs of wearing down, scale back your miles and/or take some time off from hiking. Remember, that you are at your most fragile right now. You will get to the point where you will be the hiking version of Robocop, but it will take some time to get there. Don't let your ego prevent you from achieving your goal.

The last thing you want to do is fall victim to the AT in the first two or three weeks because you were impatient. Be good to your body, you will be asking a lot of it in the months to come.

2) People who never took the emotional and psychological battles seriously

Because you've picked up this book and followed through with all of the steps indicated in the preparation chapter, you are not someone who has minimized the emotional and psychological battles. You realize that, although a half-year backpacking trip will be an overdose of fun, it's also challenging beyond belief. You're taking thru-hiking seriously. You've accepted that with the good will come the bad. You want to be prepared for when the bad happens so you can persevere. You're taking the necessary steps to do this the right way.

Not everyone is like you though.

A lot of people like the idea of a long, exciting adventure. They like to tell people that they're going to accomplish something that has a seventy percent failure rate. They're convinced they're prepared because they've spent a good amount of time outdoors. They went on a weekend backpacking trip, once. Their cousin showed them how to throw a hatchet. *They're way ahead of the game.*

Truth be told, people like this haven't put enough thought into how difficult six months in the woods really is. As soon as they are confronted with their first lightning storm, they'll undoubtedly think back to their comfy leather couch, big screen TV, and the new pizza joint that just opened down the street. They'll report back to their friends that the AT is impossible; only a madman is capable of finish such a trek.

The reality is, people like this failed before they ever left for the trail. Although they spent hours on end researching every piece of gear in their bag, they missed the mark. They prepared themselves for a physical fight, but ultimately lost the mental battle. They finally learned what you already know: comparing a weekend backpacking trip to thru-hiking the AT is like comparing stubbing your toe to birthing triplets.

In my opinion, those who drop out in the first couple of weeks (barring serious injury, illness, or other similar unforeseen tragedy) never really stood a chance to thru-hike in the first place.

Additional Considerations

Although the above reasons seem to be the most common struggles for hikers early on, there are other pitfalls to guard yourself against during this initial stretch.

3) Significant other withdrawal

This issue will be especially true if you're the type of person spends every free minute with your partner. Going from being connected at the hip to your girlfriend, boyfriend or spouse, to living without this person in the woods is likely going to be a very difficult adjustment.

If this describes your situation, you're going to have more working against you than your fellow hikers. Because I went into the trail as single as can be, I cannot give you any first hand advice. In talking to others who were going through this however, it did seem that the struggle lessened with time. They made a point to call their partner whenever in town, they sent postcards regularly, and were visited by their loved ones at least once during their thru-hike.

The times when the significant other withdrawal flared up was during the hikers' struggles on the trail. In other words, the struggle triggered feelings of withdrawal not the other way around. Because of this, it seems that the best strategy to stave off separation anxiety is to do your best damn job to enjoy the trail as much as possible – your ultimate goal anyway.

4) Sticking with the wrong group

Most people will want to hike with others, especially in the beginning. However, getting caught up in a group with whom you don't mesh well can be difficult, to say the least. Whether it's mismatched hiking paces or personalities, adding social struggles to these early stages can be the difference between loving and hating the trail. Most people quickly realize this and do their own thing or find other groups with whom to spend their time. Some, however, stick with the first group they meet. In their case, familiarity trumps compatibility.

I will address the social aspect of the trail in more depth in Chapter 5, but for now, the only thing you need to keep in mind is that you're better off by yourself than with a group you don't like. Because the AT is chock-full of truly awesome people, odds are, you'll quickly find a group that's a better fit, but this may require venturing off on your own for a bit.

Most who embark on the AT tend to be more independent and adventurous than the average person, so sticking with incompatible people is rarely a concern, although it can happen. Just remember you're in charge of making the most of your time. If something isn't working for you, *change it.*

5) Improper gear

Since purchasing the proper equipment appears to be people's biggest focus, improper gear is not the reason most
people drop out (*unless you're Mick Jagger*). However, if you
haven't done your homework regarding getting appropriate
gear, (e.g. you're starting the trail in March from Springer
Mountain and you're only carrying a forty-five degree down
sleeping bag) you're in for a world of hurt. Having proper
gear for the weather is AT backpacking 101. There's a very
good chance you're going to see snow on any given day all
the way through the Smokies, and possibly beyond. If you
don't have the right gear, you're going to be miserable.

If you haven't done your research, don't fret because
there's an excellent gear chapter in the bonus section of
this book written by backpacking gear expert, Ian Mangiardi.

Final thought

The key point of preparation in regards to this early stretch
is to enjoy the bejesus out of it. For those who are relatively
new to backpacking, this will be the most exciting part of
trail. Don't take that for granted. Live every day to its full-
est. Explore. Meet new people. Learn new outdoors tricks
from others. Take copious photos. Keep a journal to record
everything that's happening. When you read through it ten,
twenty, or thirty years after finishing the trail, your notes
will be a time machine transporting you back to this surreal
period of your life.

Because after this bliss, you are about to face a time
when, *rumor has it*, the trail begins to lose its luster. And
this is the subject of the next chapter, The Virginia Blues.

Chapter 4 The Virginia Blues

As I pointed out in the previous chapter, your first month (or so) on the trail will be unfiltered insanity. I mean this in the best way possible. Practically everything is so exciting and new that you will require little guidance in terms staying positive. Excitement has a tendency to make the hands on your watch spin a little faster. The first month will be gone before you know it. Take this as your reminder to enjoy this early period as much as possible.

Which leads me to my point....

But first, a trivia question.

Which state along the Appalachian Trail accounts for the greatest number of miles?

Okay, I probably already tipped the answer. If you guessed, "Virginia", give yourself five hundred *Badger* points[14]. You deserve it.

Of the nearly 2,200 miles that make up the Appalachian Trail, Virginia claims five hundred fifty of these, just about one quarter of the entire trail's length. And for this reason, in addition to the (mis)perception of repetitive scenery throughout the state, the term Virginia Blues has been coined.

---

[14] Redeemable nowhere.

The Virginia Blues, exactly as the name implies, is a momentary stint of depression caused by the fact that Virginia never seems to end. Hikers experience *the Groundhog Day*[15] effect whereby every morning is the same location, time, and situation.

There are two reasons why this premise is false.

First, Virginia is beautiful and no more repetitive than most of the other stretches along the trail. Grayson Highlands (and nowhere else along the AT) has wild ponies. Shenandoah National Park has some of the nicest, and easiest terrain on the entire trail, not to mention near daily access to bacon cheeseburgers, beer, and the best blackberry milkshakes you will ever encounter (these things will matter significantly more to you with 800+ miles under your belt). McAfee's Knob, a giant rock overhang whereby looking down will offer instant sensations of vertigo, is the most photographed location on the entire trail. Devil's Tooth offers the only challenging technical climbs south of the Mason Dixon line. Damascus and Waynesboro are arguably the two friendliest trail towns on the AT. I could go on.

What do all of these have in common? You guessed it, Virginia. Those who claim that Virginia is boring aren't paying close enough attention.

Also, the concept of contracting the "blues" because you're spending a lot of time in one state is absurd. The Appalachian Trail is 2,181 miles long (as of 2011). The number of state lines you cross and how frequently you cross them is arbitrary. Hiking 18 miles in Virginia gets you as close to the finish line as an 18-mile hike in Connecticut.

It's fun and encouraging to assign mini-goals along the way. Each time you cross a state line, there is undoubtedly a sense of accomplishment. I'm not suggesting you take that away from yourself. But if mini-goals are what prevent you from encountering an emotional low, who says that a state line has to be the only condition for feeling ac-

---

[15] For those who are unfamiliar, *Groundhog Day* is a movie starring Bill Murray. The movie was filmed in my hometown, Woodstock, IL. *I had to find a way to work that into the book.* End shameless plug.

complished? Every 100-mile marker is reason for celebration. Hell, every *step* is reason for celebration.

Getting halfway through the longest state is much more of a reason for a pat on the back compared to walking through all eight miles of West Virginia. If you're going to set up these mini-goals, construct them to be as encouraging as possible. Waiting four to six weeks to grant yourself the feeling of progress is a faulty mindset in my opinion.

Nonetheless, I'm not denying the fact that many hikers *do* experience a dip in spirits while walking through Virginia. It's the diagnosis that I take issue with. Those who attribute their blues to the state of Virginia are misplacing their blame. It has nothing to do with state length. It has nothing to do with scenery. It has everything to do with the death of the honeymoon.

The Honeymoon

As I told you before, the beginning of your trip is going to be chocolate-covered chaos. You will wake up in a pure state of anticipation, excited for the day's events. For those with little to no backpacking experience, each climb, each Snicker's break, each trail journal entry, each stream, every time you pitch your tent (the literal variety), will prove to be nothing short of exhilarating. Every person you encounter will embody this energy, compounding your excitement. You will think back to your former life- a time when the most exciting part of your day was broadcast on an LCD screen, inside a 12-ounce can, or was preceded by "www." In no uncertain terms, you will be in love with the Appalachian Trail, and the Appalachian Trail will be in love with you.

But, chances are, you've experienced this before, maybe not the equivalent of an extended backpacking trip, but a sense of infatuation in a different context. Maybe, it was a new relationship, an extended stay abroad, moving to a new city, the purchase of a coveted possession, the transition to a new career path, and so on. At first there is a feeling of everything being right in the world. Nothing can touch you; you've finally found a way to keep your brain saturated in a state of dopamine saturation. You walk with an extra skip in your step. You smile at strangers. You hum songs you don't even like. If there were babies around, you would kiss them. *You are in the honeymoon phase.*

And then, things change. That new car soon becomes last year's model and is no longer a source of pride. Your new boyfriend/girlfriend is beginning to reveal his or her flaws, or more accurately put, you're allowing yourself to notice them. The new city that once offered an ocean of un-limited adventure suddenly doesn't seem so big; you've been to every venue, eaten at every restaurant, and you're once again locked into your set of routines. You already know this feeling. It's the death of the honeymoon phase.

R.I.P. Honeymoon

This transition is normal. The Appalachian Trail is not separate from it. Because this typically occurs within four to eight weeks, it just so happens to coincide with a hiker standing within Virginia state lines. Blaming Virginia for your "blues" makes as much sense as blaming your middle school for puberty.

To clarify, the trail doesn't actually become less ex-citing, you just adapt to your new lifestyle. Sleeping in a tent is the new normal. Sleeping in a bed is what stands out as weird. Walking loses its novelty, *it's just what you do.*

Many interpret this feeling of lowered spirits as their cue to vacate the trail. "This just isn't as fun as it was a few weeks ago, I can only imagine how it will be in a few months from now." *If you bail out each time a honeymoon period ends, you won't ever follow through with any worth-while challenge in life.* Relationships get harder. The enthu-siasm for a new job fades. The new diet loses its appeal. For the first time, you notice the red "eject" button in your pe-riphery. Your hand hovers atop, trembling, waiting for the last straw the fall. You begin to focus on the negatives, and seek the *next Appalachian Trail* to pull you out of your rut.

So how can you avoid the Virginia Blues?

The best defense against the lull that happens at the end of honeymoon phase is *to expect it*. By reading this far into the chapter, you've done ninety percent of the work.

I'm a bit anal about the mental preparation required for major life events (thus, this book). I have an unhealthy obsession with needing to know what to expect. It's my coping mechanism. Although you can't predict everything that will be thrown your way, nor should you try, previous setbacks certainly help to prepare for each successive setback. Because I had already been through many major lifestyle changes in my life- studying abroad, going to a school where I knew no one (Madison, WI), moving across the country to a city where I knew no one (San Diego, CA), and being part of my share of "failed" relationships, I went on the Appalachian Trail overqualified for the position of "Chief of Mini-Crisis Management".

That doesn't mean you should sit around waiting for the trail to stop being fun – *that won't happen*. You're living in the woods. That's fun (source: common sense)! But, as I've stated already, it eventually becomes slightly less fun. Don't blame the trail. Don't blame Virginia. Blame human nature.

If (when) the "Virginia Blues" strikes you, take that as your cue to go back to your lists regarding the reasons you're hiking the AT. For me, when the luster faded, I found it tremendously helpful to think about what my alternative would be. Seventy-hour workweeks, undue stress, and the realization that my decompression time would likely be spent on a long hike. Perspective was quickly regained, my smile returned, and the temporary cloud of routine lifted. Your list will help you realize this as well.

The sole act of expecting the so-called Virginia Blues may be enough to douse its flames (or keep it at bay). At the very least, hopefully you now realize that this phase isn't reason enough to vacate the AT.

CHAPTER 5 HIKE YOUR OWN HIKE

I f there is one single motto that pervades the entire Appalachian Trail, it is the title of this chapter – *Hike Your Own Hike*. Although I had heard this motto before embarking on the trail, it seemed cliché and hollow. I'm guessing there's a pretty good chance this phrase is at least somewhat meaningless to you as well. What exactly does the phrase "hiking your own hike" mean? You're the one taking the five million steps, the hike belongs to you. It is *your* hike.

But there's a deeper meaning to this phrase. During your hike, you will come to several forks in the road (both literally and figuratively), and only you will know which is the correct route. These divergences will surface in the form of group dynamics, use of technology, and the *proper* amount of hiking assistance. This chapter will help you understand some of the choices you will be confronted with as well as the considerations to weigh before heading down one path versus another.

Social Dynamics on the Appalachian Trail

First Day of Class

The following section applies mostly to NOBO thru-hikers leaving between the months of March-April. This north-bound hike beginning in early spring is accounts for the largest portion of AT thru-hikers[16] Nonetheless, the basic principles in this section apply to all thru-hikers.

During the first week or two, the trail feels similar to your first day of school. Because most people go onto the AT by themselves, the majority of folks are eager to make new friends. Even a spirit independent enough to embark on a 2,200 mile hike by his/her lonesome is eager to find companionship once they step foot onto the trail. Being thrust into such a radically different lifestyle can leave you feeling a bit unsettled. The only stimulus that reminds you of your former life is that of a fellow human being. Additionally, knowing that there are others going through the same set of emotions allows you to quickly build a tight bond.

You will also come to find that many people are hiking the trail for the same or similar reasons as you. They just graduated, hate their jobs, they've hit a lull in their lives and are craving some adventure, their friend did it a few years ago and his or her thru-hike has inspired their own, they're recently retired and so on. These commonalities only serve to enhance the early stage *love-aplooza*. If nothing else, you and the person next to you have at least one thing in common: you're both bat shit crazy[17]!

It is for these reasons that group sizes tend to be rather large in the beginning. You will see groups of six to ten hikers rolling into the same campsite or shelter around the same time. You will learn how uncommon this is later on in the hike, but in the beginning, *this is the norm.*

Reality Begins to Set In

Anywhere from the first few days to the first few weeks you start to realize that perhaps you have less in common with

---

[16] *2,000 Milers.* Retrieved from http://www.appalachiantrail.org/about-the-trail/2000-milers

[17] As defined by living outside for a half year seeming like a good idea.

your hiking partners than you originally thought. A prim and proper 4th grade school teacher and 19-year-old pothead just aren't as compatible as they may have originally thought. The person you're hiking with thinks he or she is the funniest person east of the Mississippi, you feel otherwise. As nerves begin to settle, your criteria for companionship begins to grow more refined. The grouping by proximity model starts to unravel.

Soon, you'll start to consider a new criterion for camaraderie: hiking pace. In these early stages groups are still in constant flux. Since there are enough people around, you can move at whatever pace best suits you and not have to fear ending the day by yourself. You may go through three groups in a week. One group wants to press on but your legs are screaming fatigue. Another group wants to call it a day but you are still teeming with energy. Knowing that the next campsite is going be full of hikers leaves you feeling comfortable enough to do as you please. There's reassuring in knowing there will be company up ahead.

A few weeks later

On the whole, groups seem to become more stable, but injury and illness now shape a group's composition. One person in your group comes down with nagging shin splints and needs to take a couple days off. Another person drank some bad water and is a slave to the toilet for the remainder of the week. Although you feel badly and will miss their companionship, you didn't budget two days off this early in the trail. So, before you know it, the mini-parade you were marching in before is now down to two to four people.

What you lose in quantity, you make up for in quality many times over. You build very tight bonds in a relatively short period of time. Living in the woods has a tendency to strip a person down to their purest essence. There is no personality masking. This, in combination with spending several hours together every day, chatting over snack breaks, staking up your tent next to his/her hammock, and piling four bodies into a small two bed motel room, has a way of speeding up the bonding process. At no other time in life will you feel more comfortable repeatedly farting in front of someone you've known for less than a month[18].

This smaller group dynamic remains intact for a significant period of time. For some, this may last for the remainder of the trail. For most, however, they get to a point where the trail no longer arouses any sort of unsettled nerves. They've been living in the woods for a while, and they're truly starting to feel at home. It is at this point where trail's greatest motto will really begin to resonate- "hike your own hike."

Hiking Your Own Hike

There may very likely come the day where you feel at odds with your group. It may not be the result of direct conflict, although it may very well be (we'll get into that in a minute). Perhaps they need to get to town to resupply and you still have enough food to get to the following town. Maybe they want to do an eight-mile day to get to the next hostel but you still want to push further. Or perhaps you don't want to stay in a hostel because you've gone through your budget faster than you had anticipated. Up until this point, you would concede to the group's needs for the sake of your emotional comfort, but your last couple of compromises left you second-guessing yourself. You knew they weren't in your best interests. Because, by now, you've hit your "hiker stride" and have a new sense of calm on the trail, you don't require the company of others. You begin to wonder, *"What if?"*

As strange as it sounds, hiking the Appalachian Trail is a "selfish" experience. You're taking time off to do something for yourself. Although this term carries a negative connotation, in this instance, I use the phrase positively. In taking on the Appalachian Trail you will ultimately become more confident, happier person. You will gain a clearer perspective of what matters in your life. And ultimately, when you feel happier and more confident, you are better able to

---

[18] Flatulence is the universal AT language.

serve others. In this particular instance, selfishness begets selflessness.

Some lose sight of this once they get on the trail and get into a comfortable routine. The do-as-the-group-does mentality may very well be stunting their individual growth. They're afraid to break loose, not because they fear going it alone, or because they think sticking together is in their best interest, but because they don't want to hurt the feelings of people with whom they've formed close bonds.

This concern is unnecessary because leaving one's group won't be taken personally. Most hikers know that people hike the trail for a variety of reasons- to chase adventure, accomplish a monumental feat, and/or to find themselves. Going it alone offers these opportunities. Many people simply can't achieve these moments of profound introspection until they venture off by themselves. Your group will understand this. In fact, your courage may very well be the catalyst for others venturing out on their own.

> *"I love to be alone. I never found the companion that was so companionable as solitude"*
>
> *– Henry David Thoreau*

Butting Heads

It's also not unheard of to hit a breaking point with a person or people in your group. Have you ever spent six months straight with the same individual? One day together can feel like a long time. A half-year feels like three-fourths an eternity. Half of all marriages end in divorce. Hopefully, more thought and energy is put into the selection of one's spouse than one's hiking partner(s).

When a breaking point occurs you will have to choose between what's familiar and what's best for you. For most, this red flag marks the beginning of their need for independence; their own personal journey within a journey. This is the point where hikers learn who they are at their core. They see how they react to situations when they don't have the crutch of someone else making the decisions, or at the very least, providing input. This is where confidence is gained. Most importantly, when there's no one around to talk to or confer with, a calmness of mind and increased level of awareness take over your mind. Instead of being the passenger in your car, you are now behind the wheel, and you become fully attentive.

Some people never leave their group, even if they've grown rather frustrated with their hiking partners. I witnessed this in more than one of the groups around me. Toward the tail end of the trail, a fellow hiker was hit a boiling point with a couple of the guys in his group. He felt there was a gap in ethics and that some of the guys were disrespectful. Although he never liked their less than respectful actions, he put up with them. He was reluctant to voice his opinion with others, but he eventually confided in me. By this time, however, the hike was almost over. "I'm worried that I will look back at this experience and wish that I had spent more time by myself," he told me.

Don't leave the trail with regrets. Do what's best for you. Hike your own hike.

Alone, together

Although I refer to hiking the trail "alone," this is not exactly an accurate description. Odds are, you will rarely arrive at a campsite or shelter without running into other hikers. You may find that you end up with these hikers at the same shelter every night for a week straight. Perhaps you move faster than this particular group/person but you take more breaks. This can happen with a person, group, or several groups. It begins to feel like a carousel of familiar hiker faces. When it comes time to go into town and split a motel room, there is almost always a friendly hiker nearby to join you. The following day, you and your roommate might end up at different shelters, but again, you run into other familiar faces.

You will find that many others hike alone, together. You're doing your own thing most of the time, but you can still enjoy each other's company when you do cross paths. Much like the beginning of the trail, you will hike with someone for a day or two, and separate, only to meet up again as if you've never been apart.

The Story of Cayenne

If the above doesn't quite convince you of the importance of hiking your own hike, perhaps *Cayenne's* story will.

I first met Cayenne, a fellow 2011 NOBO thru-hiker, at Chet's Hostel[19] in Lincoln, NH. As a 5'11", black woman with tattoos – she stood out not only in physical appearance[20], but also due to her boisterous personality. Within forty-five minutes of first meeting her, she proceeded to get in a verbal altercation with *Vittles,* the *other* alpha dog in the room. It was at that point I pegged Cayenne as a hard-ass. It made sense that someone with Cayenne's personality type had made it this far on the trail[21] (into the Whites at this point). Her tough exterior was a reflection of her hard-nose interior- the genesis of her intense work ethic.

It wasn't until a week later where I again crossed paths Cayenne, this time in Gorham, NH. A group of us were grabbing lunch at the new barbeque restaurant in town. As is usually the case amongst thru-hikers, we cut right through the bullshit, and allow our true personalities to shine through. I was the jokester/jackass (varies with each person you ask), *Spark* was optimistic dreamer, *OB1* was the silent contemplative type, *Whoop* was the story-teller, and *Cayenne* was her normal, animated self. We got on the topic of our backpacking experience.

Immediately Cayenne's hard exterior softened.

In her best attempt to hold back tears, she informed us that this wasn't her first attempt at a thru-hike. It was very apparent that this hike meant more to her than it did to the rest of us, and not because it lacked meaning for *anyone.*

---

[19] Definitely stay at Chet's Hostel. Chet is one of the nicest guys you will ever meet.

[20] The AT is predominantly male and Caucasian. Hopefully the trail will become more diverse in the future.

[21] To clarify, it is by no means a prerequisite to be a hard ass in order to finish the trail. For every thru-hiker with Cayenne's *toughness*, there was another with a more mild mannered nature.

After finishing the trail, I reached out to Cayenne and asked if she minded sharing her experiences from her previous attempts. I wanted to know what went wrong. Here's what she said:

> *In 2008, I failed at my attempt to thru-hike the Appalachian Trail. In many ways, I was more prepared than most people out there. I spent a month on the trail in 2006. I had hiked the first 650 miles from the Southern terminus. I knew what I was getting into, but the truth is, this wasn't my first time failing at the AT. It also wouldn't be my last.*

> *My first long distance hike was cut short by 200 miles when somewhere near Blacksburg, Virginia, I had enough. I had been hiking for 4 weeks with a partner who was much faster, and I was in pain. My knees screamed on a daily basis as I hustled to complete the long days that I, mistakenly, thought had to be the norm on the trail. I was in constant hustle mode. I was not hiking my own hike. After a final sleepless night, I hiked to the nearest road and got a hitch to the nearest town.*

> *Time away gave me greater clarity. Once home, I noticed that I missed the trail. I missed the land, the instant camaraderie, and most off all-the challenge. It only took a month or two for me to start planning a "real deal" thru-hike.*

> *By the time I left Springer in 2008, I felt ready to go all the way. I was going to hike more slowly this time. In fact, this time I had a part-ner that was slower than me, so there was no danger of going too fast and burning out. There was just the danger of not hiking my own hike again. Which is where I found myself 1560 miles in and near Cheshire, MA. In the end, the official reason for my failure would be that I ran out of money.*

I did, indeed, run out of money, but I've come to understand that how much we spend as a thru-hiker is often contingent upon our psychological state. When I am a well-fed, healthy, and happy thru-hiker who is moving at a comfortable pace, I do not often get stuck in towns where I spend loads of money in order to milk what is supposed to be a brief reprieve from the mission. Don't get me wrong, I think resting in town is a good idea when needed, but stopping every chance you get can drain your budget.

Putting the trail behind me proved to be impossible. Perhaps I never really wanted to forget the AT. After all, within a year, I found myself employed at a major outdoor outfitter on the East Coast. Not surprisingly, the Appalachian Trail tends to come up quite a bit in conversation at a location like this. The fact that I had never completed a thru-hike of the AT began to gnaw at me. I couldn't let it go. I was more disappointed in myself for not finishing a thru-hike than I was about dropping out of college. Every time someone brought it up, I thought I would come out of my skin. On top of this, I had all of these trail friends on Facebook who were celebrating anniversaries. They called them trailversaries, and each one hit me hard. It became more and more apparent that I had to complete a thru-hike. Not just finish. I had to start at Springer all over again and finally walk to Katahdin. I had to go back out.

When I set out in the Spring of 2011, I was determined to finally hike my own hike. I had no partner this time. I was pretty certain that if I wasn't successful this time that I was going to be out here every other year until I got it right. The prospect of that did not sit well.

On August 25, 2011, I successfully completed my first thru-hike.

The Takeaway

This chapter is not intended to be a lecture on why you should hike some or any of the Appalachian Trail by yourself. There are those who go onto the trail hoping to find new friends, their soul mates, and/or future husbands or wives, and accomplish exactly that. There are those who go onto the trail looking for no such thing but end up with new lifelong relationships nonetheless. It happens more than you might think.

By all means, if you find a group that you really bond with, that truly meshes with your personality, don't split for the sake of splitting. If you're all on the same page about hiking pace, financial expenditure, and trail etiquette, and you feel no desire to go it alone, keep on as is. *If it ain't broke, don't fix it.*

The point of this chapter is for you to keep in mind why you're hiking the AT. In my observation, the majority of the people on the trail are independent spirits. I write this because I want you to remember that you need to do what's *best* for you, even if it's not the *easiest* option. There's a pretty good chance you'll never have another experience like this in your life. You don't want to leave with regrets. You don't want to leave wishing you had pushed yourself more. You don't want to finish thinking you didn't get as much out of your journey as possible. This path is going to look different for everyone, be sure you're going down your own.

Now that you have some insight into the social intricacies, you will need to consider another, perhaps even more fundamental, question.

What is a Thru-Hike?

On the surface, the answer to this question seems apparent: "to hike the entire Appalachian Trail in one calendar year." But *how* one hikes the hike is the subject of much controversy.

In the eyes of some, to be a bona fide thru-hiker, one must see every single white blaze on the trail. If there are two different entrances into a shelter, you must enter and exit from the same path. If you catch a hitch on one side of the road, upon returning back to the trail, you must start at the same spot you were picked up. No exceptions. If you don't see every single inch of that year's version of the Appalachian Trail, in their eyes, you haven't truly thru-hiked. Some will even claim that a true thru-hike starts at the approach trail at Amicalola Falls (which doesn't even factor onto the AT's total distance).

On the other extreme, there are those with a more liberal definition of what constitutes a thru-hike. Some people will go as far as to hitchhike past five, ten, or twenty-mile long sections of the trail. This happens often enough, in fact, that it has earned it's own trail terminology; it's referred to as "yellow blazing." In more liberal definitions, thru-hiking is more about the *experience* associated with migrating from Springer Mountain to Mt. Katahdin. The *hiking* is often secondary.

Most people, however, fall somewhere in between. The group I was with, for example, aqua-blazed past a section of the Shenandoah National Park. Aqua-blazing refers to kayaking or canoeing passed a section of the trail. Although I progressed northward for three days without seeing a single white blaze, I rationalized that I was still using manpower to get to my destination. And to clarify, this trip was nothing short of epic. Two major capsizes, lost and ruined gear, an unhealthy amount of beer consumption[22], excessive laughter, and a wonderful change of pace. Although aqua-blazing is relatively common, especially in the Shenandoah region, some consider it cheating.

The point is, there is not a single, official definition of what constitutes a thru-hike. Unlike obtaining a college degree where the requirements to graduate are clear, there are no formal guidelines to obtain a "thru-hiker" status. At the end of your trip, you have only yourself to answer to.

Of course, because of this ambiguity, some people will take it upon themselves to advocate their definition of a thru-hike. Don't take it personally, it's human nature. There is only one person you need to consult with about the

---

[22] For legal reasons, I can't condone drinking and boating. *Do as I say, not as I do.*

meaning of a thru-hike, and that is you. If you feel that a thru-hike requires seeing every white blaze, then stay true to that principle. If you want some random adventures along the way, by all means, give aqua-blazing a shot. It's your hike, hike it your way.

How to Thru-Hike

If there is no consensus on *what* a thru-hike is, there's little hope for people agreeing on *how* this should be accomplished.

Technophobe or Technophant?

For some, the idea of technology on the trail is sacrilegious. From their point of view, the trail is a sacred technology-free zone and indulging in it completely defeats the purpose of being on the trail. Even if the addition of music or a book on tape would help to make their hike a little bit easier, they opt for a more natural approach- listening to the rustle of the trees, the songs of birds, the rushing of the stream, and so forth. They might look down upon a person who carries a Kindle, MP3 player or other electronic device because he or she is relying on technology for entertainment. Those same hikers often carry a pair of books (roughly a full pound more than a Kindle – a significant amount of weight to a long distance backpacker).

I feel differently about this. Technology[23] is all over the trail. Technological advancements enable people to carry full-size tents that weigh only two pounds. I didn't see anyone on the trail carrying a six-pound tent or sleeping under sticks, mud and leaves for the sake of protesting technology. In my opinion, the line seems to have been drawn somewhat arbitrarily. Today's backpackers can carry their lives on their backs, with three days worth of food and

---

[23] Technology defined: *the making, usage, and knowledge of tools, machines, techniques, crafts, systems, or methods of organization in order to solve a problem or perform a specific function.*

two liters of water, and only be shouldering fifteen to thirty pounds. Twenty years ago, this would have been impossible. Gear has gotten more waterproof, more breathable, more durable, all the while becoming lighter every year. If you were to show Earl Shaffer[24] a modern day thru-hiker, he'd think he was watching a science-fiction movie on backpacking. So much of what is available to hikers these days would have been unfathomable just a few decades ago. *Technology* is to thank for this.

I spent a good amount of time listening to music and audiobooks on my iPhone during my trek. I love audiobooks, but rarely have the time to listen to them. I realized before departing for the trail that free time would be my only abundant supply, thus giving me a chance to finally catch up on all of the intriguing non-fiction books on tape that had been stockpiling in my iTunes library over the years. Learning the finer details of evolution *while* hiking made each wild animal encounter all the more fascinating.

Similarly, listening to music didn't take me away from the trail– it enhanced my experience. Music is art. Adding the audible pleasure of my favorite albums to the incredible scenery I witnessed added a new layer of stimulation. More importantly, stimulation was added in the areas that lacked it. There are parts of the trail that are dull and/or repetitive. If an audiobook is the difference between sanity and insanity, it's a trade worth making, at least in my opinion.

Furthermore, although the trail does offer a unique opportunity to "unplug" from the techno-craze of our society, the ultimate goal of a thru-hiker is to both finish and *enjoy* the trail. Without the aid of music and the spiritual audiobooks I was listening to during the trail, I still would have *finished* the trail, but I truly believe I wouldn't have enjoyed the experience nearly as much as I did. And remember, that *is* our goal- not merely to complete the trail, but to *enjoy it*. For me, technology contributed to my enjoyment.

Again, this is just my take. I am in no way trying to convince you to listen to music, or use technology in any-

24 The first AT thru-hiker

way while on the trail. I respect the opinion of those who feel that technology compromises their experience, I just happen to feel differently about it. If you feel strongly that listening to an mp3 player while hiking cheapens your experience, your opinion is completely valid. Just realize that it is *your* opinion[25].

Slackpacking

In 2011, a woman by the name of Jennifer Pharr Davis hiked the entire length of the Appalachian Trail in forty-six days, eleven hours, and twenty minutes, setting the new AT supported thru-hike speed record. In no unclear terms, she is an ultra-badass hiking alien robot sent from the future (or just a very determined and extraordinarily fit human, you be the judge).

In order to complete the feat of the fastest supported thru-hike time to date, she needed, well, support. *A lot of it.* Pharr Davis had a team, led by her husband, Brew (*best name ever* award) to meet her at many of the road crossings along the way and provide necessary food, water, and shelter. By not having to shoulder the weight of these supplies, Davis was able to move much faster, covering up to sixty miles in a day.

Word of Pharr Davis' legend quickly spread amongst the trail. "Forty-six days? Some people need that long just to get through Virginia. How did she do it?" Clearly carrying the same thirty to thirty-five pounds that many of us were carrying makes completing the trail in forty-six days seem unlikely, if not downright impossible. Because of this, some hikers claimed that her hike didn't count. If she didn't carry her own supplies, she wasn't participating in the same sport.

Although Pharr Davis' case is a bit extreme, slackpacking is common practice along the AT. To *slackpack* means to hike with only a daypack (lightweight pack), basically carrying only the supplies that you'll need for a shorter stretch - typically food, water, and little more -

---

[25] Just be sure to keep your technology use exclusively personal. Strolling into camp blaring the latest Bieber jam from your smartphone speaker makes you an inconsiderate jackass.

while the rest of your supplies are stored at a hostel or in a friend or family member's possession.

Although very few people receive even a fraction of the support as Pharr Davis[26], the same tactics are employed with regularity on the trail. In the eyes of some, slackpacking would compromise the integrity of their hike. For others, it's a coordinated strategy to help move them faster up the trail, no foul play associated. Until there's a strict definition of a "thru-hike", there will never be agreement among hikers, nor does there need to be. As long as you adhere to the hike that you want to have, all is right.

The Takeaway

Hiking the Appalachian Trail is a unique journey. Your experience will be unlike that of any other thru-hiker. It will be of utmost importance to keep this in mind when out on the trail. There will be those who will attempt to impose their visions of what a thru-hike should look like. They will try to pull you in one direction or another, but remember that you ultimately choose your own path.

Part of the AT experience is finding yourself. At the very least it involves gaining a better understanding. This growth will be stunted if you allow someone else to affect your decisions on the trail. Their beliefs are right, for them. Yours are right for you. They will hike their hike. You need to h*ike your own hike.*

---

[26] Covering 2,181 miles in less than 47 days is a monumental feat almost beyond comprehension. I don't care if she was carrying *negative* five pounds, that's incredible. Congratulations to Pharr Davis. Also, no, there is no relation.

CHAPTER 6 WHEN SHIT HITS THE FAN

Appalachian Trail thru-hiker fact #1: *there will come a time during your thru-hike when shit hits the fan.* It's all but guaranteed. You will hit a mental road-block. It will come paired with physical, environmental, and logistical obstacles. You will question why you're still doing what you're doing. You will struggle. You will be pushed. You will hit a new low.

Predictably, *this* is where many get pushed past their limits and vacate the trail. It simply gets too hard. They have beds, friends, family and warm meals waiting for them in their other life. Why put up with this primitive lifestyle that is full of hardship; it's not fun anymore.

There is no way around it. I know firsthand the trail has a way of testing a person.

Google Giveth, Google Taketh Away

Two weeks before leaving for the AT, I had managed to score a phone interview with a company I dreamt of working for, for the better part of the last decade- Google. *Perhaps you've heard of them?*

The image of me pacing back and forth in my bedroom while nervously answering the question, "W*hat I would do differently if I were CEO of Google,*"[27] still lives vividly in my memory. After hanging up the phone, I felt less

---

[27] For the record, this is not the position I was applying for.

than confident about my performance. I was two weeks away from living outdoors; I wasn't exactly in the right state of mind to talk business strategy, or so I rationalized.

I departed for the trail, two more weeks went by and still no response from Google. I had finally given up hope of hearing back. This was both a disappointment and a relief. I could now focus solely on hiking and not have to worry about trying to find the one spot in town where I could get enough signal to check my email.

Of course, the same day I relinquished hope, I received an email from the recruiter saying that I had passed the phone interview and that Google wanted to fly me to their headquarters in Mountain View, CA for an interview.

HOT. DIGGITY. DAMN.

I exchanged e-mails with the recruiter for another three weeks while trying to coordinate when I could get to a town that offered shuttle service to a nearby airport. Most of the towns along the AT are no bigger than a few hundred people, not exactly mass-transit hubs. Furthermore, as you will learn, trying to predict when you'll arrive at a particular destination two hundred miles away is a guessing game, at best. Terrain, weather, and day-to-day energy levels are variables in constant flux.

This was no easy task. If it were any other company, I would have politely declined. *But this was Google.* I had no choice but to follow through.

I remembered that my friend from college, Mitch (yes, the same anti-Tony Robbins from Chapter 1), has a sister, Jill, who lived in the trail town, Damascus, VA. Because Jill wins *the greatest person on earth award*, she offered to drive me to the Tri-Cities airport in Tennessee, an hour away.

My brief trip to San Francisco was nothing shy of surreal. I had been living in the woods for over a month at this point. Other than my few hitches into town, I didn't move faster than four miles per hour. I was now driving a rental car around a city I had never been to, while mentally gearing myself up for the biggest interview of my life- for which I was *greatly* under-prepared. Because the only clothes in my possession were my trail garments, I met up with a college friend, Brandon, to borrow his suit. I drove back to the luxury hotel paid for by Google, and immediately passed out in my king size bed. *Score.*

I woke up after my first *full night* sleep in a long time and dedicated the next couple of hours to catching up on all the major technology news I had missed over the previous five weeks. I showered, pounded a cup of coffee, and began my drive to "The Googleplex[28]".

As I shut the door to the rental car, I caught one final view of myself in the reflection of the car window. *"Homeless clown"* was the first thing that came to mind. To say that the suit I had borrowed fit awkwardly was putting it lightly. Brandon is 6'2". Badger is 5'11". I looked like an eight-year-old who had broken into his dad's closet to play dress up. Additionally, because my already extra-wide feet had flattened out an additional size while on the trail, there was a *zero percent chance* of my fitting into his shoes. I had no choice but to rock my bright blue *Hi-Tec cross-trainers* into this interview. Add a month of fantastic ginger-beard growth, and you have correctly envisioned me- the *homeless clown.*

After checking in at the front desk and quickly sucking down my blueberry Odwalla smoothie[29], a very casually dressed guy in his early thirties strolled out and looked around the room. *"Zachary Davis?"* I stood up, shook his hand, and was escorted back to a large conference room overlooking a nicely landscaped grass lawn where many of the very intelligent looking Google employees retreat during breaks.

Four half-hour interviews flew by in an instant. *"Estimate how much Ad Revenue Gmail makes in the United States in a single day." "Tell me how much profit is made from the Droid App Store in a year." "How many automechanics are there in this country?"* Huh? Math? *No one said anything about math.*

Some of my answers felt pretty good. Some were laughably bad. I walked out feeling like I had just finished a twelve round championship fight. I got back into my car

---

[28] Google's headquarters.
[29] There was an entire mini-fridge stocked full of these expensive smoothies, on the house, of course.

and started driving back to the airport, trying to process what had just happened. Although a month in the woods had *drastically* calmed my nerves, the business portion of my brain must have been covered in Snickers residue. *Bluntly put, I had calmly delivered unimpressive answers.*

I returned to Damascus the very next day and got right back onto the trail. I had officially thrown in the towel regarding landing a job with Google. *"Now I can finally focus on my hike."* I was merely trying to ease the pain from what I anticipated to be bad news from the recruiter.

Three Weeks Later

I got an e-mail from the recruiter asking to give him a call the next time I was in town. *I was in town.* I called him back immediately.

"Zach, I just wanted to let you know that the feedback I received from this end was excellent. *Congratulations* - *y*ou have passed the face-to-face interview."

I was in disbelief. No way was this happening. I was in the midst of the biggest adventure of my life, and just found out that I had all but received a job offer from the company I would gladly sell my soul to work for. My spirits settled softly somewhere in the stratosphere. "All we have to do is submit your application to the hiring committee and we'll finish the details from there," the recruiter added.

The next opportunity to get to a computer and complete the lengthy Google application wasn't until I arrived at the Holiday Inn in Daleville, VA, another couple hundred miles north of where I had received the good news. The computer I used was either one of the first fifteen machines ever built or it had contracted all known computer viruses. *I could have finished the rest of the trail in the time it took to open Microsoft Word.* Regardless, I gathered all the required pieces and sent my application to the recruiter.

Over the course of the next two weeks, my mind bounced between the trail and San Francisco, mostly favoring the latter. I was planning what borough of the city I wanted to live in, how to get my possessions across country and which of my friends I could coax to move out there with me. When it came up in conversation, I was quick to boast of the job waiting for me on the other end of the trail. I texted those closest to me and let them know where I was landing in October. What seemed like an impossibility was now my reality.

The next contact I received from Google was the following e-mail, from the recruiter:

> *"Apologies for my delay, I was in meetings all afternoon. I did hear back from the hiring committee earlier today and unfortunately, I don't have good news.*
>
> *They did not approve your application and as a result, we are not able to make you a formal offer at present time.*
>
> *I don't have any specific feedback, as they don't share this with us regarding hiring decisions.*
>
> *I know this can be frustrating and I'm happy to schedule a call for early next week if you would like to discuss in more detail."*

I reread the email fifteen more times to make sure I wasn't misunderstanding something. *I wasn't.*

Wait...*what*!? I had passed both interview rounds, and *now* I'm getting turned down? This must be some sort of sick joke. To add insult to injury, I don't even know why I was being turned down (*still to this day*).

The entire interview process began prior to my leaving for the Appalachian Trail. I got *that* news in Harper's Ferry, approximately half way through the trail. I had spent the first half of my hike grasping onto the slim hope that I had a job with Google waiting for me on the other end.

Now what?

I was devastated. I proceeded to isolate myself from everyone around me. I camped alone. I avoided conversations at all costs. I needed space to process the disappointment. This was easily the lowest I had felt since stepping foot on the trail.

And then it got worse.

From bad to worse

Within a week, I started to get severely debilitating headaches. I assumed that perhaps they were merely a result of the stress that I had just been through. I told myself to give it a week and the headaches would go away.

Three weeks later, not only had the headaches not dissipated, they were far worse. I went to the hospital in Harrisburg, PA, suspecting that I had contracted Lyme disease (my biggest fear going into the trail). The results came back negative. The doctor wasn't exactly sure what was causing the headaches, but because temperatures had been reaching into triple digits, she suspected dehydration was the cause. She told me to drink more water and sent me on my way.

Three weeks later, despite the increased fluid intake, the headaches persisted. Additionally, not only did my head throb, but I was experiencing blurred vision on occasion. My moods were inexplicably sour despite my finally coming to grips with the Google debacle.

I was reaching exhaustion several hours earlier than I was used to. Twelve mile hikes over flat ground felt equivalent to a twenty-four mile day through the more challenging Virginia terrain. "How could I be getting in *worse* shape?" It didn't make sense.

I knew I had to go back to the hospital. This time a family member picked me up and took me to the emergency care unit in White Plains, NY. Again, the test for Lyme disease came back negative (apparently, it can lie dormant in your system for quite some time before registering positively). I got a CT scan due to my fear that the tension and visual disturbances were the result of a brain tumor. Luckily, they weren't.

The doctor proceeded to run a series of other tests, including a screening for other tick bites and blood infections, all returning negative. Again, since the test results revealed nothing else, the doctor suggested that I was battling dehydration. He urged me to intake more sodium and drink an electrolyte supplement as regularly as possible.

I followed the doctor's orders to a "t." I carried a salt shaker, dumping a couple teaspoons in my mouth every hour or two, and had my very, very, very worried mother send an expensive electrolyte supplement as often as possible. For about a month, this seemed to cure my ills. Unfortunately, however, the headaches came back, albeit less frequently.

Upon finishing the trail, since I would no longer be hiking ten-hour days, I assumed the headaches would subside. I was wrong. In fact, the headaches got worse. The first two weeks after summiting Katahdin, I was couch-ridden, on a diet of aspirin and misery.

It wasn't until one month after summiting where additional blood tests revealed that I had contracted West Nile Virus. Apparently the neurological effects of WNV can be long lasting. I wasn't able to get a concise answer from any doctor as to how long I could expect to battle headaches.

As of today, the headaches do still occur, but far less frequently and intensely than before.

Turmoil, From the Outside and In

There I was, still more than *1,000 miles* from my intended destination, battling the biggest emotional let down of my life. Less than a week went by and I contracted West Nile Virus, a rare virus known to kill those with weakened immune systems. Injury was added to insult, literally.

As surprising as this might sound, I can say with 100% honesty; *exactly zero part of me ever considered getting off the trail.* Call it determination, call it stubbornness, call it stupidity; I set out to do something, and *damn it*, I wasn't getting off the trail until it was done.

This stubbornness/stupidity/determination isn't a result of some biological trait. I know this because I was not

always this way. I learned and applied strategies that en-
abled me to stay the course, both physically and emotionally.

In the next chapter, I will share these strategies and
show you how you can prepare for when the shit hits your
fan.

CHAPTER 7
CONQUERING OBSTACLES

As we learned in the previous chapter, I was dealt a pretty nasty hand during my thru-hike. Although my case was a tad extreme, it was also far from the most extreme. A fellow 2011 thru-hiker, *Wildcat*, endured plantar fasciitis, pneumonia *and* Lyme disease- and he finished the trail (yeah, *holy shit* is right). Although you shouldn't anticipate quite so much shit hitting your fan, know that encountering obstacles is a matter of *when*, not *if*. Coming to grips with this fact before you actually encounter the roadblocks is a crucial component to persevering.

I have mentioned more than once already, a surefire way to deal with the challenges that lie ahead is simply to *expect* them. For example, in *The Virginia Blues Chapter*, I reminded you to expect your love affair with the trail to eventually lessen. Although the emotional fallout from a honeymoon phase ending can be a real challenge for some, the obstacles addressed in this chapter are on a whole other level. *These* challenges put the Virginia Blues to shame.

The challenges I refer to are contracting Lyme disease, West Nile Virus, or Giardia. It's breaking your leg, getting shin splints, or having a layer of blisters cover the bottoms and sides of your feet. It's severe loneliness, homesickness, or boredom. It's finding out that your girlfriend/boyfriend has found someone else. It's finding out that your income source, for whatever reason, has gone dry.

It's having your pack stolen from right under your nose. This challenge- is *your Appalachian trial.*

This is the point when the next wave of hikers decide they've had enough. They could endure the rain, cold, heat, and insects. These are all elements of the trail; they were expecting it. The sprained ankle, however, they were not prepared for. They tell their trail friends that they're going home to rest and will rejoin the trail in a couple of weeks. They don't return. The sprained ankle tested their resolve and they failed.

Many of those who don't throw in the towel here are the most stubborn, determined individuals on the planet. Although the trail is an ongoing struggle for them, in their eyes, they have two choices: summit Katahdin or die trying.

I don't want you to throw in the towel. I also don't want you to struggle excessively. So then, how can you have your cake and eat it too?

Is Your Drive Driving You Crazy?

Having drive plays an important role in *finishing* the trail, but it does little in terms of *enjoyment.* The tactics outlined in the *Mentally Preparing* chapter are in place to help you craft this drive. You already know my mantra- I don't want you to finish the trail if it means you'll dread the process. Thru-hiking the Appalachian Trail is meant to be an enjoyable adventure. No one is paying you to do this. You're doing this for *you.* The reward is solely intrinsic.

That said, not every day on the trail will be fun. If approached correctly, however, you will be able to sport a smile on the days when you'd otherwise be drenched in despair. At the very least, you will be able to keep a positive outlook whereby you might otherwise fall victim to chronic negativity. Once the record in your head gets stuck on, "*this sucks*", it's hard to get on to the next song. So, let's flip the album over onto its other side.

The following are mindsets that will help you keep a cool head in the face of turbulent times. They're what got me through a demolished ego and West Nile Virus. These aren't intended to build drive (although this might very well be an unintended consequence). These tools offer a way to reframe your *obstacles* into *opportunities*. In addition, these outlooks are in place to help you avoid the most common pitfalls hikers fall into when presented with the more severe challenges.

The following frames of mind are not my thoughts exclusively; they represent a compilation of the best advice I received from others who have endured similar journeys, including Ian Mangiardi, introduced in the first chapter, as well as other successful thru-hikers from the class of 2011. Some of these suggestions will resonate more with you than others. Adopt what works; disregard what doesn't.

Five Mindsets for Unwavering Mental Endurance

1) If you try to beat the AT, the AT will beat you

We are naturally competitive creatures. If you're in competition with another person, it is your goal to do everything within your power to try harder and outdo their efforts. When you do, you succeed. On the AT, however, when dealt a tough day, week, or even month, gritting your teeth and hiking longer days or increasing your pace will have the opposite effect. Put bluntly, pushing harder in the face of struggle is how hikers burn out and ultimately fall off.

If your car's caution light goes on, the proper response is not to ignore the signal and slam the gas pedal to the floor. Similarly, if you're having a bad week and can feel your mind's caution light switch on, get your ass off trail at the next opportunity. This signal happens for a reason. Without proper maintenance, a hiker's trail vehicle (his/her mind) will eventually falter. There's no shame in taking a day or two off to get a breath of fresh air (figuratively speaking, of course).

Odds are, after a couple of days of greasy fast food, bad television and the confining feeling of too much time indoors (this will make more sense to you once on the trail), you'll soon remember why you got on the trail in the first place. Also, remember this is an ideal situation to consult your lists, as it will immediately bring you back to your pre-trail psyche.

For some, this reminder may occur after only a couple of hours. For others it may require a couple of days. Take as much time as you need to get yourself sorted out. If you have a bad week, take a few days off. In your nine-to-five world, your boss might not be so understanding.

Those who fight against this feeling (or ignore it altogether), are marking the beginning of their end. At best, they're suffocating any possibility for enjoyment.

Now repeat after me: *"If I try to beat the Appalachian Trail, the Appalachian Trail will beat me."* Good.

I'm aware that there are those who don't have the luxury of taking as much time as they want in town. They're either on a strict schedule or tight budget (even though there are ways to decompress on the cheap). If this is you, the next point will carry more weight.

2) Don't just roll with the punches, embrace the punches

It was December 2008, my final semester at the University of Wisconsin-Madison. My first class of the day started at 7:40 a.m., roughly four hours earlier than my body naturally *turns on*. The day's high was *negative* eight degrees, and with wind chill, it was *at least* ten degrees colder than that. I begrudgingly walked to my Black Music and American Cultural History course (seriously). In front of a half-filled lecture hall, the first words out my professor's mouth were, "It's days like today you either have to embrace the weather, or go completely mad."

This is the sort of mentality we need to adopt.

To take the "Don't fight the AT" point a bit further, instead of fighting against what the trail hands you, take the obstacles as they come. It's part of the experience. Embrace the challenges, or go mad.

Keep in mind, what we term as a "challenge" is entirely subjective. There are no universal challenges per se. It's the meaning we ascribe to events that makes them *good* or *bad*, insurmountable challenges, or opportunities to grow our character. What we call "reality" is really just an interpretation of events based on prior life experiences.

So if reality is a byproduct of our perceptions, it's our job to rewire how we perceive tough times. We need to look at the glass as half full.

When hiking in the rain, for example, instead of wishing that it were a sunny day, make the most of what is given to you. Smile. Sing. Splash in puddles. If you find yourself missing friends and/or family, instead of spending time wishing you were with them, embrace your current situation. Focus on growing tighter bonds with those that are already nearby. If you're by yourself, embrace the calmness seclusion offers. It's a rare circumstance that you can get quality alone time in the secluded woods. There is profound wisdom to be gained in these situations. This will elude you if your energy is spent wishing you were spending time with others. Remember, the glass is half full. See the water, not the absence.

If you can't embrace what's happening, you should at the very least *accept* what's in front of you. Wishing that your day were anything other than what is, is the fastest path to dissatisfaction. It may sound overly simplistic, but there really is great power in acceptance. In finding peace with what is, you will notice a sudden weight lift from your shoulders and your struggle will dissipate.

3) It's a Marathon, not a sprint

More accurately put, it's like 83 marathons.

There was a common sentiment amongst many of the hikers I talked with toward the end of the trail; they were fairly ready to be done. Although most weren't to the point where they were dreading the process, there was a little more purpose behind their gait. They picked up speed toward the end of the trail rather than savor the process. Of all the advice I acquired before leaving for the trail, this is the one piece I failed to heed. I learned firsthand why savoring the process is important. I will explain more about this in the next chapter. I hope you can learn from my mistake.

4) This too shall pass

It's as cliché as it is profound.

We have a tendency to get lost in the content of the world around us. If one is suffering from muscle pain in his/her leg, there's a tendency to frame this as "I am in pain" instead of "there is pain in my leg." *What's the difference?*

Surprisingly, a lot. When we confuse our existence with the content that surrounds us, we lose the boundary that separates the two. We confuse the content for *who we are*. The pain is a personal attachment. *I* and *pain* are inseparable. Because this is the case, it's all that we can focus on. Subsequently its effect on us grows infinitely. Our attention lives in the pain, and the pain becomes the frame through which we seen the world.

There is a simple yet deeply transformative solution to this dilemma. *Space.*

By telling yourself that *this too shall pass* you can create this space. Here you are reminded that there's a gap between *what is happening* and *who you are*. You are reminded that, like everything else in life, the conditions are only temporary. You realize to not lose yourself in the moment because the *only* constant is change.

Rainy days, freezing mornings, and sweltering afternoons are all bound to happen on the AT. This simple mantra can cease to make you the victim and instead make you a spectator. You will see the light at the end of the tunnel. Presence emerges and the conditions outside of your control are no longer a cause for struggle.

5) Challenges are opportunities for growth

I could've just as easily entitled this section "everything happens for a reason," but there is often a loss for *what* that reason might be. In my opinion, this frame of mind more clearly highlights the opportunity that can result from your obstacles. For me, *this point was the single most important strategy in overcoming challenges.* I want to emphasize this point. This isn't a tactic only for enjoying yourself on the Appalachian Trail. This is a tactic for *making life your bitch.*

I'm guessing you probably know people who possess a "Woe is me," victim-like attitude toward their daily existence. No matter what's happening around them, they're only focused on what's going wrong. Regardless of their circumstances, life is out to get them. Because of this, they develop a defeatist attitude- "Why bother? It never seems to work out for me anyway." The interesting thing about these people is that they are 100% correct. Whatever mentality you adopt will eventually manifest itself.

> *Whether you think you can or can't, you're right.*
>
> - Henry Ford

> *As long as a man stands in his own way, everything seems to be in his way.*
>
> - Ralph Waldo Emerson

The AT is chockfull of challenges. It is up to you as to whether or not you use these to your advantage or disadvantage.

Walking through a lightning storm won't just better prepare you for the next lightning storm. Knowing you survived one unnerving situation will calm you the next time another one arises. When you overcome an illness on the trail, it will make the next injury seem less severe. Each challenge on the trail better prepares you for the subsequent one.

But of even greater importance in becoming better equipped and more confident *on the trail* is the way in which it will benefit you *off the trail.* The lightning storms will help you keep your head in what would otherwise be perceived as a tense situation at work. Being injured or sick on the trail will give you more appreciation for your big, comfy bed, Nyquil, and On Demand television. Crushing through The Great Smokey Mountains while battling a severe case of blisters will obliterate your former standard of working through the pain. Rolling your ankle prior to a 1,500 ft descent through freezing rain will put your *bills* into perspective. Finding peace in times of solidarity will remove loneliness from your lexicon.

Inevitably, completing a journey as monumental as a 2,200 mile backpacking trip will leave you feeling invincible. When you get through this, is there anything that can touch you? *Hint: no*, there's not. You'll leave the trail feeling like Alonzo Harris, Denzel Washington's character from the movie Training Day.

"King Kong ain't got shit on me!"

It is precisely these challenging moments that you will reference as a source of personal strength to rise above *any* obstacle in life. For me, all daily tasks, no matter how *serious* they may be, now pale in comparison to battling excruciating headaches, 100-degree temperatures, and a crushed ego. The little things that used to normally irk me: traffic, a negative interaction, suboptimal weather and so on, seem to have lost their ability to rattle me. *At least I'm not dodging lighting.*

Remember, the obstacles in front of you are there for a reason. This is your test. This is your opportunity for growth. Again, look back at your lists, and rediscover what it was that you wanted to get out of the trail in the first place. Is it possible that these challenges are granting you the opportunity to acquire these traits? Are you going to struggle against it? Can you look your obstacle in the eye and laugh? Can you inspire those around you with your unflappable mindset? This might very well be the greatest challenge in your life. *What do you want to remember about the way you handled it?*

Again, I want to remind you that *welcoming* the trail's hurdles will help you accomplish the ultimate goal: to maximize enjoyment. You're going to be on the AT for a long time, equip yourself with a mentality that favors joy over struggle. You'll thank yourself when all is said and done. This I promise you.

Presence, the greatest present of all

Sometimes a positive mindset is hard to maintain. After a tough day at work, a fight with a loved one, or other form of unexpected bad news, one's mind has a tendency to head into a dark place. You should all but expect unexpected bad news on the trail.

The methods mentioned previously in this chapter are frames of mind. I realize that it's difficult to get back into a good place without actively *doing* something to make this happen. If switching from a negative frame of mind to a positive were as easy as reminding yourself that "challenges are opportunities," world peace would have been achieved by now.

Sometimes *action* is required to remedy the negative body chemistry that comes from an unforeseen hardship. Some turn to drugs, alcohol, food, sex and so on. Not only are these much harder to come by on the trail, but they ultimately compound the issue(s) at hand. Some choose to talk their issues out with others, and while this can be beneficial, you also risk it backfiring if your confidantes are going through similar difficulties. You can sink further into a hole.

What are we left with? *Exercise*? You already do that, *a lot*.

For me, meditation was a cure-all.

There is no shortage of benefits from meditation. "Neuroscientists have found that [those who meditate] shift their brain activity to different areas of the cortex – brain waves in the stress-prone right frontal cortex move to the calmer left frontal cortex. This mental shift decreases the negative effects of stress, mild depression and anxiety. There is also less activity in the amygdala, where the brain processes fear."[30]

Additional claims of meditation's benefits include an enhanced immune system, cured headaches, increased energy, decreased muscle tension and more.

So what do I mean by meditation?

The American Psychological Association defines meditation as the following:

> *Meditation is used to describe practices that self-regulate the body and mind, thereby affecting mental events by engaging a specific attentional set.... regulation of attention is the central commonality across the many divergent methods.*

Even by this definition, it's clear that meditation has a variety of meanings, but a central component involves the "regulation of attention". In order to accomplish this, one needs to find a setting with limited distractions.

What better place void of distraction than the middle of the woods?

The following are meditation methods I used while on the trail. They represent a variety of meditation/spiritual readings I've done over the years. It's in your best *interest to* research meditation literature for yourself, as I do not claim any expertise[31].

In all, meditation sessions should take about thirty minutes to an hour. If you're having trouble harnessing your attention when first starting out, try shorter durations, maybe ten to fifteen minutes. As is the case with anything else, the more you practice, the easier it becomes.

I can assure you that I was horrible at meditating when first starting out (years ago). It's normal to get caught

---

[30] Allen, Colin (April 2003). *Pyschology Today.* Retrieved from http://www.psychologytoday.com/articles/200304/the-benefits-meditation
[31] If you're going to pick up only one book, make it A NEW EARTH by Eckhart Tolle and reread it as many times required for it to *click.*

up in the repetition of your thoughts. Don't get discouraged if/when this happens. Gently let go of the thought and pull yourself back into the meditation without getting down on yourself.

1) **Find a quiet place** with comfortable seating (on a log or flat soft ground) at least 100 ft off trail to avoid getting distracted by other hikers.

2) **Sit upright** to allow your lungs to expand and contract completely.

3) **Close your eyes and begin to breathe deeply**. Use a ratio of 1:4:2 for inhaling, holding your breath, and exhaling, respectively. For example, inhale for a count of four, hold your breath for a count of sixteen, and exhale for a count of eight. You can change the length of your breaths and exhalations as long as the ratio remains the same (e.g. 2:8:4). Do this repetition for five to ten minutes.[32]

4) **Begin body awareness meditation**. Gently move your attention away from your breath and into different areas of your body. Focus your attention on your toes, feet, ankles, knees, thighs, stomach, chest, shoulders, arms, hands, fingers, neck, face, and head. Let your attention move sporadically throughout your body. Your body will let you know where attention is needed.

5) **Begin positive intention meditation**. Take time to recount all of the things in your life for which you're grateful and or appreciative. Feel the love you receive from friends and family. Once you're in touch with these feelings of gratitude or love, practice the body awareness meditation exercise described above. Focus that energy in the places that have stored stress or tension.

6) **Slowly open your eyes** and quietly observe your surroundings. Observe without judgment. Focus your full attention on a minute detail of your environment: a branch, a rock, a leaf, an insect and so on.

---

[32] For more breathing meditations and exercises, I highly recommend looking into Dr. Andrew Weil's work.

You may vary the steps in this mediation or do any portion of it. I used the above format on a fairly regular basis to clear my head. Play around with different techniques to see what works for you. Meditation such as this lightens the burden of the issues weighing on your mind. Sometimes they evaporate completely.

Typically, I meditated prior to lunch to avoid competing with the digestion of food. You want as much free energy as possible. If you're really hungry it might help to eat something small beforehand. Try not to overdo it, as blood will rush into your stomach, causing distractions. If the middle of the day doesn't work for you, practice meditation when you can to find a time that does work. If you find it easier to do it upon waking or right before you fall asleep, by all means, do that. There's no such thing as a bad time.

I also found it helpful to practice meditation *while* hiking. This requires a conscious shifting of focus out of your head and into your body and/or breath. While walking, spend ten minutes letting your attention wander to the strength of your legs. Then dedicate the next ten minutes to focusing only on the natural inhalation and exhalation of your breath.

This can be an extremely effective way to short circuit a negative thought pattern, thus restoring joy into your day. Additionally, this is an easier meditation to work into your routine. You're already walking- now you can multi-task. Finding time to break without eating or socializing requires much more motivation and self-control. Even if you practice this for only fifteen to twenty minutes a day, you will find that you feel more energized than you were prior to the movement-based meditation.

One final point – it's in your best interest to start practicing meditation *before* hitting the trail. This is true for two reasons. One, it will be helpful to have experience in meditation so you're not discouraged when you get lost in your thoughts while trying to meditate on the trail. Two, meditation is amazing. The best time to meditate is always *now*.

CHAPTER 8 SPRINTING MARATHONS

"If you could do one thing differently during your hike, what would it be?"

T his is the question that I have received more often than any other since returning from the Appalachian Trail. It's a fair question, although a difficult one for me to answer.

This is the case for two reasons.

One, I don't believe in regrets. Human beings are prone to making mistakes. You show me someone who doesn't make mistakes and I'll show you a lying bunghole. Learning from mistakes grants us the opportunity for improvement. The only regret that should coincide with a mistake is a failure to adapt.

Two, I would hate to admit that I would change anything about my experience. It was the best half-year of my life. Even the hard times have ultimately turned me into a better person.

As much as it pains me to say this, there is a section of the trail that I wish I would've approached differently.

Please, pay attention to this chapter. Learn from my mistake.

The Whites

From the moment you step foot onto the AT, you will hear of the infamous mountain range in northeast New Hampshire referred to as the Whites, short for White Mountain National Forest. People will tell you of the near-vertical ascents and descents that extend beyond forever. People will warn you of how the weather will turn from divine to dangerous in the blink of an eye. People will tell you of the confusing camping options, "You can stay at the huts, but they're expensive, unless you get in for free, but if they're full, you can't get in, but then you can stealth camp, but there's no where to stealth camp." "*What??*"

You know what? They're right (at least for the most part). The Whites are majestic, a hot bed for inclement weather, pose a somewhat confusing array of sleeping options, and above all, they are difficult.

By the time you get to The Whites, your hiking ego will be running at an all-time high. You've just walked through twelve of fourteen states. Every state since New York has gotten increasingly more difficult, and you're still crushing out big mile days. "Bring on The Whites! People are just fear mongering," you'll tell yourself.

I told myself this.

Turns out that it wasn't just fear mongering. Hiking through the Whites requires a humbled approach in the face of your heightened hiking prowess. Once you reach the Whites, it's as if someone flipped the difficulty switch into the "on" position. The climbs become two or three times longer than what you're used to, and all of a sudden, the term "switch-back" leaves the trail lexicon. Although you've been adjusting to the increasing difficulty for the last six hundred miles, give or take, this stretch seems to skip a few rungs on the ladder.

When you hear suggestions to drop your hiking pace back to the twelve to fourteen mile range, it's not because twelve miles will consume your whole day, it won't; it's because your legs will feel exhausted at this point (clearly, the exact mileage will vary from person-to-person, but the onset of fatigue will occur much sooner than it had prior to this point). You've seen climbs similar to the Whites in short bursts, but nothing with this duration. Because of this, you're exhausting a whole new set of muscles. In essence you're starting over. These specific parts of your legs and joints aren't trained to the point where you can hit the ground running, figuratively speaking, of course.

For the sake of clarity, you shouldn't fear the Whites (or any part of the trail for that matter). Although The Whites are more challenging than the terrain to the south, this stretch is nothing short of magnificent. The increased difficulty doesn't translate to a decrease in fun. Conversely, it can and should be one of your favorite, if not *the* favorite, part of the trail! You'll have several mile-long stretches above tree-line, granting you panoramic views of the untouched, lush New Hampshire landscape. Such scenery quickly lightens the perception of a heavy workload.

My Mistake

I somehow convinced myself that once I hit the Whites, I was on the homestretch. On paper, it made sense: 1,800 miles down, only 400 to go. Eighty percent of the trail was behind me. I was *already several strides down the last lap*. I'd be standing atop Katahdin before I knew it. Or so I thought.

I was definitely not alone in this feeling. Although some waited until southern Maine to grant themselves permission to feel that they are were hitting the home stretch, this premature declaration was undoubtedly a common theme. Others would plan their exact summit dates in order to meet up with friends and/or family in Baxter State Park. They would ambitiously predict their average daily mileage to make this happen. "Well, I only have to do sixteen miles a day to finish by the 24th, that's nothing."

To be clear, sixteen miles through the Whites and southern Maine is tough as fuck. Making predictions about this last stretch is a dangerous guessing game. If you're going to try to meet up with others in Baxter, I urge you to err on the side of a conservative hiking pace.

Mountain Range Musical Chairs

The Whites have an interesting set-up whereby thru-hikers can exchange their labor for lodging (called "work-for-stay") at the huts run by the Appalachian Mountain Club (AMC). To the average weekend warrior, these huts are as minimalistic as it gets. A few wool blankets, a bunk bed, a toilet and running water. No shower, no private bedrooms, no lighting, no heat, no outlets, definitely no flat-screen television.

To a thru-hiker, however, the huts are as luxurious as one could ask for. Two large, hot meals (dinner and breakfast), indoor shelter (typical sleep accommodations are the dining room floor), running water, and a small library. Hikers are happy to exchange a little bit of labor for the aforementioned benefits, even after an arduous day.

There is one caveat, however. Each hut typically only takes in four to six hikers per night, and operates on a first-come, first-serve basis. If you get there too late or too early, they'll either point you to the closest stealth camping spot or tell you to hike on to the next hut. It seems as though the cutoff for getting there too early is anytime before 4p.m., show up after 6p.m., you're too late. If you get there between 4-6p.m., odds are you'll get one of the few thru-hiker spots, although *still*, not always. The one exception to this is the Lake in the Clouds Hut, which is not only much larger, but because it's just south of Mt. Washington with it's volatile weather, the staff is less likely to turn NOBOs away. It's simply too dangerous to do so.

This system essentially results in one giant game of musical chairs. I vividly remember planning my entire day around trying to get to a particular hut around 4p.m. Because I wasn't used to the increased difficulty of the terrain, and subsequently, the reduced hiking pace, I always underestimated how long it would take for me to get to my destination. Because I was determined to be one of the lucky few to get a spot at a hut for the night, I ended up pushing myself, taking far fewer breaks than I otherwise would have. My days amounted to six to seven hours of intense climbing and descending with only a few breaks above ridgeline to absorb as much of the beauty as possible. I passed weekend and section hikers as if they had shackles on their legs whereas I had springs in mine. Although I always accomplished my goal of getting one of the few AMC thru-hiker work-for-stay spots, I soon realized that a couple of free meals wasn't worth the daily stress of racing through the Whites. I would show up drenched in sweat, often chafing, and usually miserable. Needless to say, I got worn down pretty quickly.

Despite the physical fatigue from the increased demand of the Whites, I was determined to continue my increased hiking pace. I was, after all, on the last lap. The finish line was in sight, no time to let up now. Although I predicted that I would finish with an empty tank, at last I would *finally* finish. The other side of the trail promised real food, a soft bed, reunion with friends and family, and most importantly no more headaches (or so I incorrectly presumed). My brain drowned out the screaming of my knees. "I can almost see the finish line, just a little further..."

Being four hundred miles away from a destination is too far to begin a countdown on any stretch of the trail. This mistake is *exponentially* more costly when hiking through the Whites.

The end of the Whites symbolized relief, as I was now only a couple dozen miles away from the NH-ME border. Upon reaching Maine, the terrain would become more forgiving. *"I'll be able to hit my stride once again, and, alas, Katahdin will be mine!"*

Maine-tained Difficulty

Again, I was wrong. Maine is in no way forgiving. It's every bit as challenging as the Whites, and in certain stretches, even more so. The scouting report I received from others regarding this final state was mixed. Most, however, were telling me what I didn't want to hear: "Southern Maine is hard." Through the practice of selective listening, I convinced myself that the worst was behind me upon crossing the NH-ME border. "I've been sprinting for 10 days now, just a couple more weeks to go!" A *couple* weeks, ultimately turned into *three*.

One of the things about sprinting, is that it gets increasingly less fun the closer you approach exhaustion. Your body is screaming: "STOP IT, DUMMY. *I'm making you feel shitty for a reason.*" I heard the message my body was sending all too clearly, but still I pushed.

As I approached each trail town in Maine, I could feel my spirits lift. Although I knew this was my cue to grant myself a break, I refused to do it.

I went into Rangeley, with a pair of trail friends, OB1 and Spark to celebrate the former's 21st birthday. The next day, in the face of a potent hangover, sore leg muscles, and stiff joints, the others decided to spend the day in town to recoup. My legs were telling me to do the same. My head, however convinced me to keep pushing. So, *I pushed.*

Soon thereafter, I arrived at Stratton to pick up the electrolyte supplement Mother Badger had sent her dehydrated son. Just down the street was the Stratton Motel, a fair-priced hiker hostel. My legs were telling me to check in for the night. My head won once again. I did some laundry, threw a cheeseburger and ice cream cone down the cheeseburger and ice cream hole, and immediately hitched back onto the trail. *I pushed.*

By the time I arrived to the road into Caratunk, I was with seven other hikers. We had gotten word of the Kennebec River Brew Pub, which offered handcrafted beer, bar food, and a hot tub. *Of course we were going.* After a few beers and a burger, five of the seven hikers decided to set up camp there for the night. It was the smart move (for their bodies, but not so much for their wallets), but of course, again, I pushed.

When I got to Monson, I was a zombie. This time, not taking a day off wasn't an option. After all, Monson is the town on the south end of the 100-Mile Wilderness- a 100-mile stretch intersected only by a few logging roads. If I sustained a serious injury or breakdown in any way, there was no assurance of rescue. I had battled exhaustion for three weeks, so this was especially worrisome.

In hindsight, not taking a day off could have been a dangerous decision. Even with this extra day of rest, the only thing pulling me through the 100-mile wilderness was the promise of my long-awaited prize on the other end. Each climb seemed to add more weight to my pack. If this were any other 100-mile stretch, I might very well still be walking through it.

My energy level skyrocketed once again as I scaled Mt. Katahdin, arguably the most challenging climb of the entire trail. Upon returning to the park headquarters at the mountain's base after the highly anticipated and very emotional final summit, my adrenaline levels plummeted back down to earth. There was no more masking what my body was telling me. The fuel tank was empty, and had been for quite some time. The 20-yard walk from the park's picnic table to our shuttle back to reality was every bit as difficult as the previous steep five-mile ascent to glory.

The Takeaway

There is a saying on the trail that once you are eighty per cent of the way through the AT, you have expended only twenty percent of your effort. Although this is a bit of an exaggeration, the meaning behind the statement is on point. The increased output in effort over the shorter distance will result in a decrease in daily mileage. Again, this will vary from person to person. Your body will let you know. Please, listen.

You may be thinking, "Yeah, you pushed yourself, but you finished sooner than you would have otherwise without incurring injury, or any major setback. Is there really a lesson to be learned from this?" Although this is true, the drawback from pushing yourself through fatigue in the Whites and Maine is that it takes a toll on your emotional state. Those who exercise regularly know that there are days where you're dragging through your workout. Whether your muscles are drained or you're working with insufficient sleep, your thirty minutes on the treadmill seem to last for hours.

In small doses, this feeling is manageable. When your sole task in life requires a high level of demand from your body, however, it's detrimental to your overall wellbeing. Odds are, when battling illness, you aren't your normal cheery self. Although my symptoms from WNV were mild at this point, my energy level resembled that of someone who was ill. By the time I had crossed into Maine, which is arguably the trail's most beautiful state, I was under-appreciative of the magnificent terrain I was living in. Because of this, I cheapened my experience.

A Promise to Yourself

This struggle is avoidable. I realize now that I failed because I had broken my own rules. *Learn from my mistake.*

I looked ahead. I tried to sprint a marathon. I tried to beat the Appalachian Trail. Not surprisingly, the Appalachian Trail beat me. Fortunately, because I was so close to the finish line at this point, the idea of quitting never entered into the equation. But, because I was too focused on my destination, my appreciation of the journey lessened in the process. As you will learn for yourself, the journey is what matters.

Upon reaching the Whites, make yourself the following promises:

1) **I will not look ahead**. As the mileage remaining draws ever closer to zero, this task becomes increasingly more difficult. You will have the mindset of a ninja at this point; stay strong. Katahdin will come, but don't look past what's in front of you; it deserves your full attention and appreciation. *Right now* is the only time you'll ever have, and in regards to this stretch, it should be a damn good time.

2) **I will go into the Whites and southern Maine with a sense of humility**. You're a hiking machine. You're in the best shape of your life. You've been kicking the trail's ass for the better part of four months or more

to this point. But the Whites are a new game. You'll have no problem handling the terrain, but crank it back a couple of notches. Start off slowly because, once you hit the Whites, it'll be a while before you see easy terrain once again. If you feel your body starting to wear down, give yourself a day off. Listen to your body.

3) **I will not attempt to sprint a marathon**. There will come a time when you feel as though you can push the gas to the floor. You'll attempt to exhaust your fuel tank at the same time you cross the finish line. Trust me, the payoff from doing so pales in comparison to the penalty you will pay for mistakenly attempting this too soon. At best, you'll finish a couple days before you would have otherwise. More likely, because you'll be battling exhaustion, you'll end up finishing at the same time, if not later. You will also fail to maximize your enjoyment of these few precious remaining days. Although you'll probably be looking forward to returning to civilization, keep in mind, cross-country strolls don't happen every day. *Soak up every last drop.*

By making these promises, you will put yourself in the best position to finish the trail strong, both from a mental and physical standpoint. Odds are, you're going to have a lot of eager fans on the other side of Katahdin, more than you might think. They'll want to know about your adventure and it'll take energy to accurately convey what you've gone through over the previous half-year. Leave some fuel in the reserve tank for this purpose.

SECTION THREE:
POST-TRAIL

CHAPTER 9 LIFE AFTER THE APPALACHIAN TRAIL

C ongratulations! By this point you will have just completed what once seemed incomprehensible. You'll have backpacked from Georgia to Maine, a true lifetime achievement! You'll wear your thru-hike like a badge of honor for the rest of your life. Nothing or no one can take that away from you. Others will look up to you as an inspiration, with admiration. You set out to do something bold, and damn it, you'll have done exactly that! The next time you tell someone you're doing anything, they'll think twice before doubting you. You're as crazy as you are ambitious. You will now be introduced to others as "that guy/girl who backpacked 2,200 miles". Be prepared, *you'll have a lot of questions to answer.*

But of greatest importance, you will have proven to yourself that you are capable of *colossal* achievements. You will utilize this confidence to propel yourself onto monumental feats in all other facets of your life. There is no challenge too big for you to take on.

Unfortunately, you will have almost no time to take a break before the next challenge slaps you in the face. In fact, for some, this next challenge will be every bit as daunting as your cross-country trek. This challenge, unfortunately, will bring no accolades or heroic worship.

What I am referring to, of course, is your reintegration back into society.

On the trail, you will very likely develop a fresh, new perspective on life. Over the course of a half-year you have adapted to a radically different lifestyle. You will have given up your modern luxuries, and simultaneously shed the layer of insanity that pervaded your life. A half-year without the media circus, ubiquitous advertising, and menial daily drama has a way of shedding new light on your way of thinking about everything.

Your life will have been reduced down to focusing on survival and finding joy in life's simple pleasures. Stress occurs only in situations when it's warranted: running through a hail storm, unexpectedly stumbling upon a rattle snake or baby black bear, or conserving enough body heat through the night to avoid hypothermia. Now the concept of a deadline, *who* said *what* to *whom*, and concern about physical appearances are totally irrelevant.

You will have reached a purer, more natural state of existence.

But eventually, you'll be on a one-way flight back to your former world. *What will you do?*

The Adjustment

There's no easy way to put it, transitioning back to your previous environment will be a difficult adjustment. Like many of life's more challenging moments, the best medicine is time. But also, much like our experience with "The Virginia Blues," knowing what to expect can help ease this tough transition.

Taking this a step further, there will be stages you can expect to go through in your post-hike world. I will describe the stages of my own post-trail adjustment, as well as share the insight I've gathered from other thru-hikers the input I've gathered from other thru-hikers.

Stage 1: Toto, We're Not in Kansas Anymore

You've just finished something that you have poured your heart and soul into nearly every day for the last half- year (and even longer than that when taking your preparation into account). And then all of a sudden, one day you wake up and you're done. There's no more goal to walk toward. However, it'll still take a few days for you to even realize anything is askew. Physically, it'll merely feel as if you're taking a *zero*[33]; it's no different than your normal trail routine. Mentally, although you'll know that you've reached "the end," it won't yet sink in. "I'm done. *What does that even mean?*" you'll ask yourself.

It won't be until around day three or four that you will know you've landed on a new planet. Your former world was amidst trees. *What's the deal with all of these walls?* The biggest adjustment will be going from ten hours of activity a day to being relatively sedentary. The constant inhalation of fresh mountain air was invigorating beyond words. Now, all of a sudden, it's gone. Last week you were running on an endorphin high. Today, you'll battle through an endorphin deficit.

Stage 2: The Post-Appalachian Roller Coaster

You will vacillate between growing comfortable in your new life, and longing for the old. You'll see some of your old habits in a new light. The people and places you left behind feel different, and somehow exactly the same simultaneously. As you look around, little things will remind you of life on the trail. You'll daydream back to a place where you measured time by the position of the sun instead of the digital clock on your office desk. At the same time, you'll remind yourself that you were clamoring for this life at various points toward the end of the trail. In other words, expect to be confused- you'll be up, you'll be down. You won't be quite sure where you are or where you're going. Some days it will feel like you're lost, while others will feel as if the previous half year was merely a dream.

---

[33] Trail terminology for a day off.

Stage 3: Getting Back on Track

Every day will start to get better. You'll now begin to look back at the Appalachian Trail with a healthy nostalgia instead of an envious longing. The confidence that you acquired through your *Appalachian trials* and tribulations will begin to surface in other facets of your life. You'll start to develop momentum in a new direction, whether it's in planning your next adventure, your professional career, or becoming involved in a new relationship. You're starting to reach stable ground. The fog will lift.

Stage 4: In the Flow

It is at this point that you will have started the next chapter of your life. You will now fully utilize the self-efficacy that comes from achieving something as colossal as backpacking the length of the country. You'll settle into a routine that works for you. As you look back at the trail with admiration and nostalgia, you will realize that the next adventure is simply a decision away. This will bestow you with a sense of freedom. You'll realize that life *really is* your oyster. Whatever you invest your time and energy into will come paired with a new vigor and uncompromised determination.

But it's in these early stages that former thru-hikers struggle with most. Despite the euphoria that comes with monumental accomplishment, many hikers experience an inexplicable feeling of depression on the other side of the Katahdin. I was fortunate to have heard about this phenomenon long before completing the trail. I want to share what I've learned with you.

Advice from Miss Janet: Post Appalachian Trail Depression

It was a warm summer day and a group of twenty plus hikers huddled around a large picnic table in the backyard of the Happy Hiker's Hostel in Glencliff, New Hampshire. The night's menu offered home-cooked meatloaf, grilled corn on the cob, mayonnaise laden pasta salad, coleslaw, home-made buns lathered with liberal amounts of butter and, of course, Miller High Life. Hungry hikers were shoveling plate after plate of delicious homemade fare directly into the deepest part of their throats. It was as if we unlearned the art of chewing. A week of consuming only Ramen noodles can do that to a person.

This particular homemade meal marked a special occasion. The hostel culture typically requires a hiker to fend for him/herself. The Happy Hiker Hostel is no exception. But on this evening, we were graced with the presence (and culinary skills) of Miss Janet.

Miss Janet is an Appalachian Trail celebrity. I remember my first week on the trail, a fellow hiker (with whom I had never conversed), approached me and excitedly said, "Did you hear that Miss Janet is hiking the trail this year?"

"Are you serious," I asked, "Also, who is Miss Janet?"

Apparently that was a dumb question (my forte). A legend of the trail (having been featured in the popular AT documentary "Trail Angels"), Miss Janet, has been involved with helping AT hikers for more than thirty-five years. Miss Janet's hostel in Erwin, Tennessee was regarded[34] as arguably the best hiker hostel on the entire Appalachian Trail (in competition with more than sixty others). Some hostels are known for their cheap rates, some are known for the quality of their accommodations. Miss Janet's was known for, well, Miss Janet.

That's why, when Miss Janet talks, hikers listen.

We were in the midst of devouring said meal when Miss Janet chimed in, "Hey y'all, I know you're enjoying your dinner, but I've got a couple of important points I want to get across to you."

The first was, after we get off the trail, *expect to get fat.* We laughed and quickly nodded in agreement. For obvious reasons, our appetites resembled that of a pregnant di-

---

[34] As of 2011, Miss Janet had closed down her hostel, although look for her to be *guest hosting* at another hostel in the immediate future.

nosaur's. There was little doubt our eating extravaganzas would soon catch up to us.

The second issue elicited a change in her tone. As she grew a bit more somber, Miss Janet began to discuss what was a common post-trail scenario: *hiker depression*. It was at this point you could look around and see more than twenty contemplative faces as they took to heart Miss Janet's predictions. Apparently, she had struck a chord. Others had likely anticipated what Miss Janet offered, but her words made this premonition all the more real.

Although I had heard some word of post Appalachian Trail hiker depression during my stint on the trail, I was unsuccessful in finding any concrete information or advice online. Realizing that I had a rare opportunity to pick the brain of one of the most knowledgeable AT minds alive today, I asked Miss Janet if she would be willing to discuss this topic in more depth.

She obliged.

I had the fortune of videotaping our discussion. If you'd like to watch the full interview (and you should), please visit: zrdavis.com/2302

The takeaways from our conversation are as follows:

- **Eat Well**: I'll cover this issue in more depth later in the chapter, but one piece of advice I can offer you is to look into nutritional testing after the trail. Spectracell (www.spectracell.com; $99) is a leading provider of this type of testing. A Spectracell test will give an in-depth analysis of any nutritional deficiencies that you may have developed while on the trail. By obtaining this information, you will get a better idea of which foods to introduce into your diet to re-establish proper nutritional balance.
- **Stay Active**: As I alluded to earlier in the chapter, the biggest adjustment from trail life to post-trail life is the change in your activity level. Part of the change in mood seems to stem from a change in body chemistry. Exercise produces endorphins, the feel-good neurotransmitter, endorphins. It's possible that the

feelings of depression stem from the drop in endorphin levels. Although this theory is only speculative, keeping active does seem to help. Therefore, I'm sticking with it. In general, making drastic changes in your life causes changes in how you think, feel and in your body's physiology. To suddenly cut back dramatically on exercise, a drug, a relationship, or leaving a familiar and psychologically comforting setting can result in "withdrawal symptoms." You will likely be exhausted after finishing the trail, and therefore uninspired to do anything active. But keep in mind, even light exercise can help.

- **Stay Connected**: Keep in touch with those who you've befriended along the trail. Although other friends and family will be there for you upon your return, they simply can't relate to what you're going through and what you've gone through (unless they've embarked on a similar life-altering journey). The friends you've gained during your journey on the AT will be there to remind you that you're not going through this transitory phase alone. By discussing what you're going through with trail friends, your issues will feel normalized, thus helping you get beyond this temporary low. They will be your best support.

Your Next Appalachian Trail

There is another reason I believe that this depression can occur. For a half-year, you have been moving toward one single goal. There was no question about what you were going to do on a given day. The answer was clear- *walk toward Mt. Katahdin*. You were working toward something tangible. Although it may have felt like adding drops of water in hopes of creating an ocean, you knew that eventually you would obtain your goal. Finally, after five to seven months, you could see the finish line. All of that time and effort had finally culminated in your prize.

Suddenly, the first day after the trail, there is no prize to work towards. Much like the withdrawal of endorphins, you're experiencing a withdrawal of purpose. This can be avoided.

Before getting off the trail, spend time plotting your next adventure. Some will interpret this as another backpacking trip, or similar outdoor vagabond journey. It can be this sort of adventure, but doesn't have to be.

For me, this book was my next Mt. Katahdin. The first day sitting in front of my keyboard felt a lot like stepping foot onto Springer Mountain; the finish line seemed to be light-years away. I knew there was a final destination to move toward. Much like the AT, I struggled to find the motivation to keep myself in front of my computer as often as required to write a book, but as I approach the finish, I am reminded of the importance of setting and reaching for goals. It's what gets people out of bed in the morning.

What is *your* next Appalachian Trail? Dedicate some time to really consider what inspires you. It shouldn't matter how crazy the idea seems, nothing can be crazier than walking from Georgia to Maine. You will have done that. You will have proven to yourself and others that you can do whatever you put your mind to. *Go do it.*

I realize that some people have trouble identifying what that next journey should be. For me, I find meditation to be a great resource for digging to the core of what I should be doing with my time. If you're having trouble finding something to feel passionate about, prior to meditating, set an intention of "Why am I here?" and meditate on that mantra. Don't struggle to find the answer, the answer will find you. Just be present enough to notice when it emerges.

If this doesn't help you find something inspirational enough to move toward, make a conscious effort to start learning new subjects. Order a few new books from Amazon. Take a new class. Talk to those who inspire you and ask what new ventures they're getting involved in. Find out what's available on the World Wide Opportunities of Organic Farms website (www.wwoof.org). Watch fascinating TED Talks (www.ted.com). Send me an e-mail, I'll be happy to help you figure it out. You will likely surprise yourself with how quickly you can uncover inspiration.

Post-trail weight gain, an inevitability?

When Miss Janet pronounced that we would get fat upon finishing the trail, I wasn't surprised to see the lack of opposition to her prediction. Although my fellow thru-hikers looked like skeletons with beards, we had been shoveling *multiple* plates of comfort food into our faces.

As it turns out, Miss Janet was putting it lightly. I reached out to former thru-hikers after finishing the trail, and the feedback I got was rather interesting. Not only do a lot of hikers put on the weight they had lost over the previous five to seven months, many end up doing so twice as fast as they had lost it. A good portion even tack on more weight than they had originally lost. And this weight gain occurred even when people resumed normal, non-AT, eating habits.

I found this to be curious. A half-year of endurance exercise and junk food must do something to a person's system that creates this post-trail weight gain. If they're determined enough to bust their butt for a six months, poor self-control post-trail seems to be an unlikely explanation for why many lose the battle of the bulge.

I researched this subject to learn what those who were able to keep their weight down after the trail were doing differently. To my surprise, I was unable to find any relevant information on this topic.

Unsatisfied with making only slightly educated guesses as to why this occurs and what thru-hikers can do to prevent it, I reached out to Nathan Daley MD, MPH. Dr. Daley practices integrative preventive medicine and performance medicine at the Leonardi Institute (www.leonardiinstitute.com) in Colorado. I specifically wanted to know if the weight gain was an inevitable consequence of going from extreme endurance exercise back to a more moderate activity level.

There is good news: Dr. Daley doesn't believe that post-trail weight gain is inevitable. Staying at a healthy weight will take some work, however.

The following tips are Dr. Daley's advice on what you can do to prevent post-trail weight gain:

7 Tips to Avoiding Post-Appalachian Trail Weight Gain

1) Prioritize low glycemic foods on the trail.

Low glycemic foods tend to have moderate to high fiber, fat, protein and water content. Non-starch vegetables are the classic example, but these are not easily packed for hiking. Drying anything (fruit or vegetables) increases the glycemic index/load. So reduce consumption of dried fruit, granola, crackers, candy bars and sweets, and increase consumption of nuts, whole fruits and vegetables, lean meat sources (jerky, etc.), and even a fiber supplement (a small pack of Metamucil). For hikers experienced in the local edible flora and fauna, harvesting some wild edible plants is a good way to consume low glycemic foods with fiber. Just be careful, many seemingly edible plants are poisonous.

It might be helpful to know that not ALL dried fruit is a problem. Dried apricots and dried apples have low glycemic measurements and are acceptable, but raisins have a high glycemic index and load and are not acceptable. Low glycemic bars made of nuts and dried fruit may be convenient to have on the trail as well. I recommend KIND bars.

Additionally, studies show that low glycemic foods are the best for maintaining blood glucose and replacing glycogen stores in endurance athletes.

2) Prioritize protein while on the trail.

This will help prevent weight loss and will help keep satiety mechanisms in place (protein, fat, fiber all contribute to a sense of satiety).

3) Let your return to civilization also be an entry into a new lifestyle.

Commit to a new nutritional plan. Retain a diet focused on low glycemic foods (vegetables, meat, eggs). This keeps insulin levels low and prevents fat storage. Have this as your plan before even starting the AT in order to avoid fantasizing about starchy comfort foods like bread, pizza, burgers, french fries, etc. while you are on the trail.

   The AT changes people, but then civilization changes them right back. By committing to a better lifestyle once back from the AT, you remain in control and, in a way, your AT journey never really ends.

4) Prioritize protein, lean meats (fish, chicken, buffalo, elk, etc.), in addition to low glycemic vegetables upon return.

This allows lean muscle mass to return instead of body fat and satiety mechanisms can help control portion size.

5) Try very hard to continue being physically active at a high level.

By this, I do not mean maintaining a sixteen to twenty four mile a day regiment, but take a regular five mile hike, swim, walk, run, cycle, do yoga and so on. It is fine to take three to five days off at first, but have a plan to stay active and fit. Active recovery (even light exercise) is better than passive recovery (sitting). Taking light walks the day after you return can help you recover faster. High intensity exercise (intervals, etc.) is best for keeping body fat low and building back lean mass.

6) Begin contemplating or planning your next adventure.

Start planning your next adventure to avoid the post-Appalachian Trail blues. Start to dream. This will help you feel upbeat which will help get you in the mood to start exercising again.

7) Useful post-trail supplements.

There are a lot of supplements you can introduce into your diet to help you regain a healthful nutritional balance including fiber (acacia, psyllium, arabinogalactan/larch tree, glucomannan; all good options), probiotics (20+ billion CFUs of bifidobacterium and lactobacillus species), omega 3 fish oil (2-3 grams of omega 3 fatty acids daily), whey protein powder (Solgar Whey to Go- it is a non-contaminated brand-used to reach 70-110 grams of total protein a day depending upon body weight), and MCT oil (medium chain triglycerides; thermogenic fats which help maintain a high metabolism).

An example of a day's diet under Dr. Daley's plan would look something like the following:

> **Breakfast**: 2-3 eggs, spinach, ½ cup lentils
> **Snack**: Protein shake (30g of protein in 12 oz. water)
> **Lunch**: Fresh greens salad with 6 oz. of chicken breast, ½ avocado, olive oil or balsamic vinaigrette dressing.
> **Snack**: 1 cup of Greek yogurt with 2-3 oz. blueberries
> **Dinner**: 8 oz. salmon, steamed greens

If you're unfamiliar with the principles of a low-glycemic diet, three books I highly recommend are, THE SOUTH BEACH DIET, THE PALEO DIET, and THE FOUR HOUR BODY. The first two are focused solely on diet, while THE FOUR HOUR BODY covers a wide range of topics, including diet and exercise, but also sleep techniques, sex, and injury prevention.

Don't underplay the value of eating a healthy well-balanced diet after getting off the trail. Eating nutritionally dense and low-glycemic foods will go a long way in improving your sense of well-being and to keep all those hard-earned pounds off.

Summary

The preceding tips are unlikely to entirely prevent the momentary low associated with finishing the Appalachian Trail. See your blues for what they are. You will have just finished something truly awesome. There is going to be a let down from anything of that magnitude. Remember, *this too shall pass*, and when it does, you will like what follows- a new and improved you.

CHAPTER 10 THE END: YOUR NEW BEGINNING

I was less than ten days from my much-anticipated summiting of Mt. Katahdin. I had been hiking by myself for a couple of days, rarely crossing paths with others. That's why I was caught off guard when I saw a pack of seven NOBO hikers huddled together on the trail ahead. This wasn't a logical rest area. They stopped on the slope of a hill, in a location lacking scenery or any inviting seating. I slowed my pace and continued toward the group. I was listening to the new My Morning Jacket album for the ninety-fifth time when one of the hikers, *Drum Solo*, started walking slowly in my direction. *Drum Solo* is the type who always sees the good in life and for this reason, a smile is permanently affixed to his face- *except in this instance.* Something was askew. As I pulled out my white Apple earbuds, he said, "Dude, you're not going to believe this..." he hesitated, *"there is a dead body ahead on the trail."*

Fifty-one year old, Michael Guerette- trail name- *Open Mike*, was hiking south from Katahdin, (part of his SOBO thru-hike) when he hit the ground on a moderately sloped downhill portion of the trail. A pair of hikers, *Squirrel* and *Bluegrass*, were close enough to hear his body make contact with the ground. Initially they thought it was a deer, but as they approached, they saw Open Mike's body lying motionless just off the trail. They called the police, and followed instructions to resuscitate him, to no avail. *Squirrel* and *Bluegrass* believed that he died upon impact, possibly before. Certainly, judging from the lack of color to his face, he was gone by the time I arrived.

The whole scene was surreal. The other seven hikers and I sat and waited by Michael Guerette's body for forty-five minutes so we could fill out witness reports when the local authorities arrived. In the meantime, we contemplated the weight of the situation. Most, myself included, sat there in silence, in disbelief. What do you say after something like that? *What can you say?* Others offered their theories as to what happened. A couple of hikers attempted to crack jokes. It was apparent that they did *not* find humor in the situation. *They were uncomfortable*; they didn't know how to handle themselves. Aside from bodies that had been embalmed for a funeral, none of us had seen a dead body before. Needless to say, we were all rattled, even those who wouldn't readily admit to it.

The next few hours were a blur. The vision of Open Mike's body consumed my thoughts. My mind entered into a different world. I kept thinking of how easily that could have been any one of us. If it was in fact a simple fall that caused Open Mike's death, then there was no good reason to think we weren't all susceptible to such a tragedy. I began to recall the times I had gotten my foot caught on a root while hiking a steep descent, only to have made a dumb luck recovery, allowing me to narrowly escape serious injury. I recalled the times when I had actually face planted into the ground, only to notice a large, jagged rock on either side of my head. Over the course of five million steps, even if you're 99.99% accurate, five hundred of those steps are going to be bad. Was Open Mike a victim of the .01%? I had always wondered how NFL football players get back on the field and run into each other at one hundred miles per hour after watching one of their teammates get carried off the field on a stretcher. I was now confronted with an even more challenging scenario. It was here that I learned the answer; you do it because you *have to*, not because you *want to*.

Worse yet, I began to think about all of his family and friends. I was upset because I saw the body. *I didn't even know the guy*. I immediately felt worse when I thought about all of the people who just lost a loved one forever. *A world of sadness can spread in an instant.* This was the *only* thought on my mind for the next few miles.

Needless to say, I wasn't much in the mood for hiking.

It wasn't until four hours after originally seeing Open Mike's body that I gained some perspective.

Upon reaching the next shelter, I sat down and flipped through the trail log to see if Open Mike had entered anything.

He had.

His last post was a detailed entry about how great it had been to encounter a family of hikers heading in the opposite direction. He talked in great depth about how fond he was of the youngsters in the group, and that he hoped that they really enjoyed the remainder of their hike. He said it was a great pleasure to make their acquaintance and that it made his day. And then there was his sign off....

"Today is a great day to be alive. – Open Mike"

Still to this day, this thought gives me goosebumps.

The takeaway

Although Open Mike's passing is undoubtedly a truly saddening story, I feel that we all should be so lucky to go the way that he did: doing something he loved, lavishing unconditional kindness upon strangers, and being the recipient of love from countless others.

Which brings us back to my original point: hiking the Appalachian Trail is meant to be enjoyed. *All of life is meant to be enjoyed.* Open Mike was doing it right. The simple, routine interactions with others "made his day". For him, every day was a great day to be alive, even his last. We never know when our last day will be, but this is of secondary importance. It's what we're doing with it that matters.

And in order to make the most of everyday, we need to take responsibility for what's in our control, and surrender to that which is not.

What's outside of our control? *The elements.* Lighting will happen. Soreness will happen. Sweat-soaked clothes will happen.

What is within our control, however, is much more profound than any amount of precipitation, it's our perception. Life will supply you with all of the play's props, but only you are able to write the script.

Open Mike was exposed to the same storms that ultimately send seven in ten hikers home. The difference between those who succeed, and those who do not, however, is the story they tell themselves in this process. By this standard Open Mike was successful.

You will soon learn for yourself that hiking the Appalachian Trail isn't about arriving at Mt. Katadhin. Katahdin is a sweet bonus, a symbol of your accomplishment, and a fitting *finish* to a truly epic journey.

Instead, hiking the Appalachian Trail is about each and every of the five million steps along the way. *This is the single greatest takeaway you can leave the AT with.* This mindset will not only ease your struggle, but will ultimately make your entire experience far more enriching.

Similarly, life isn't about achieving a certain income, "making it" to retirement, or buying a certain house. *Like the AT, life is about each step along the way.* The learning lessons from the Appalachian Trail will bring this profound truth into focus.

Don't take a single moment for granted and, like Mike, live each day as if it were your last.

When you finish hiking the Appalachian Trail

I don't have any children[35], but I feel a fatherly pride in you. Your finishing the trail is of sincere interest to me. When you picked up this book, I told you that I feel responsible for helping you accomplish your goal- becoming a successful thru-hiker. I have taken that commitment seriously.

When you do finish, please, let me brag about you! I want to know about your journey. I want to know what about this book worked for you. I want to know what didn't. I want to know your personal story. Please, email me all of your *Appalachian trials* and triumphs at theGoodBadger@gmail.com.

Additionally, be sure to send me your pictures from Katahdin! I want to see the success painted across your face. I want to share your photo with others. Again, email your Katahdin photos to theGoodBadger@gmail.com. I will share your photo on a dedicated successful thru-hiker page on my website (www.theGoodBadger.com) to celebrate your triumph with the world!

From the bottom of my heart, thank you for reading this book. I eagerly await hearing the story of *your* journey.

---

[35] That I know of

Section Four:
Bonus Material

Gear, Deer ticks, and Everything in between

CHAPTER 11 IAN MANGIARDI'S GEAR CHAPTER

T his book was written under the assumption that you've already spent ample time researching your gear needs. That being said, judging from the wealth of questions I receive from readers of my site, it's quite clear that gear is people's number one concern. Although I've stated repeatedly that the key to thru-hiking the Appalachian Trail lives more in your mind than in your pack, what's in your pack *does* matter. To neglect this topic would be doing you a disservice; I am here to serve you. And for me to be of *best* service on this particular topic, I have called upon Ian Mangiardi to do the heavy lifting.

As I've mentioned several times throughout this book, Ian served as my pre-trial mentor and therapist. He was gracious enough to share his best insights in regards to keeping a strong mindset on the trail.

That said, if asked, Ian would readily admit that psychology isn't his top backpacking related strength. As someone who has thru-hiked both the Appalachian Trail and the Pacific Crest Trail (and will undoubtedly earn his triple crown in thru-hiking the Continental Divide Trail within the next couple years), Ian is a self-proclaimed *gear junkie*.

With more than 5,000 miles of backpacking experience under his belt, Ian has turned his passion into a career. His website – thedustycamel.org – is a haven for all
things gear related[36]. He eats, breathes, and sleeps the
stuff. Don't tell him I said this, but quite frankly, he suffers
from gear OCD (look for GOCD in the next DSM issue).

Ian had final say in every piece of equipment I took
with me on the trail. I put all of my trust into his expertise.
I'm glad that I did. Having the guidance of someone like
Mangiardi in planning for a backpacking trip is like having
Bob Vila offer a lending in hand while building your first
cabin. In finishing the trail, I ended with essentially the
same gear that I started with. Ask any successful thru-
hiker - this is quite an impressive feat. I attribute 100% of
this to Ian's thorough and concise advice. If he was able to
take someone who knew *nothing* about recreational equipment, and within a short time have his pack fully prepped
for a successful 2,181-mile journey, I'm confident that you
too would have much to gain from his guidance.

It is for this reason that I asked Ian to share his wisdom with you. He was gracious enough to write a thorough
summary and provide you with the same advice I was
granted on how to pack for thru-hiking the AT.

Lastly, be sure to check out the Appendices of this
book as it includes the full gear checklist as approved by
The Dusty Camel.

Without further ado, I am extremely pleased to present you Ian Mangiardi's Gear Chapter.

Appalachian Trail Gear: What You Need to Know

There is a vast world of gear out there, and it is easy to get
hung up on how much everything weighs- counting each
gram, ounce and pound. However, the first thing to realize
is that with each additional ounce usually comes an ounce

---

[36] Also look for his new PCT documentary "The Walk Home". I got a
sneak peak; it's going to be awesome.

of comfort. It's easy to get your pack weight down below ten pounds, but what is not easy, is getting a lightweight pack that keeps you contented for months on end. After thousands of miles of trekking with nothing more than what is on my back, I have found that I'd much rather carry the extra pound if it means I will sleep soundly.

The AT is a unique trail, with a similarly unique set of gear requirements. It's hot half the time, cold the rest, and all the time: wet. Gear's toughest adversary is moisture. Whether it's rain, humidity, or falling in lakes, any moisture will kill a piece of gear. For this reason, the Appalachian Trail is one of the most brutal treks in terms of gear longevity. So how do you trek over two thousand miles without destroying your stuff? You don't. Most of the gear you purchase will, in fact, be destroyed by the end of the trail.

For the past three years, I have worked in the outdoor gear industry, and I can say this industry is probably the most kick-ass. People are relaxed, the companies are cool, and the solid brands know what's up. If you call any one of the major quality brands from the trail, explaining that you are a thru-hiker and one of their products broke, they will go out of their way to make sure you get a new piece.

Why is this?

In any industry, products are marked up between three to five times the actual cost, so when a thru-hiker calls about a failed item, the company is still making money even if they replace it, on the house. The benefit for the company comes largely from the testing, and subsequent marketing. Who better to test the limits of equipment than people in it for the long haul? No one else is really relying on the product for thousands of miles, nearly half a year of tough work. Thru-hikers can see what breaks first, the weak points in the products they choose. A positive experience with a company – be it through quality products, efficient customer service, or hopefully both – can garner lifelong customers.

As anyone who hikes a long distance trail knows – everyone LOVES his or her gear. It's an actual relationship. If people don't love their gear, hikers inform the companies and then gear gets replaced quickly. The gear companies love the feedback. Why not trust the opinion of a thru-hiker? The reason this book probably ended up in your hands is because you respect the opinion and experience of thru-hikers. Take advantage – respectfully – of the relationship between thru-hikers and the gear companies they select. And don't feel bad about giving companies input and asking for what you need because they benefit from this as much as you do.

With the understanding that your gear is essentially "insured" during active use, pick your gear accordingly. Spend the extra fifty bucks, and get the nicer piece. This will not only guarantee the quality, but will also likely be correlated to weight. The heavier pieces will be less expensive, where the lighter pieces mean newer, more costly technology. The lighter weight pack will undoubtedly be the pricier pack.

Now for the big number – what can you expect to pay for this super comfortable, lightweight pack? You're looking at a two- to three-thousand dollar pack. Yes, that does seem like exorbitant amount of money for a backpack full of things, but think about how long you plan to rely on that gear. Six months worth of rent will run you *at least* three thousand dollars, so why shouldn't your pack be similar? It's your living expense.

Once you accept that intimidating number, then the fun begins. Research, purchasing, and testing. Depending on your personal level of nerdiness, you can spend as little – or as much – time as you like planning your gear. The industry is ever changing, and the newest lightweight exciting piece is always changing as well– so, do your research. Nerd out. Create an Excel spreadsheet and program it to automatically update the end price and weight. Round to the nearest ounce (not gram) and overall pack-weight in pounds. This will give you an easy number to understand (pounds), but more specific numbers to work with on an individual item level (ounces).

A spreadsheet will keep you organized, give you your exact pack weight, and give you a quick link to the specs on each piece. The best way to break it down is by categories. The big five are: clothes, food, water, luxury, and miscellaneous. Keep in mind, your overall pack weight is going to be EVERYTHING you own. A big portion of that gear is going to be worn, thus not part of your actual pack weight. You can get fancy and exclude your daily use items if that works better for you.

Here, I will share with you what has worked for me in over five thousand miles of long distance hiking.

The Big Five

This consists of your tent, pack, sleeping bag, sleeping pad and footwear. Having faith in these essential items is invaluable to a successful thru-hike.

Tent

A lot of people hike the AT without a tent. This is something I would never do. You have no privacy, are bound to shelters and must sleep right next to everyone – and anyone – around. If you hike the trail in prime season, you don't need a fancy mountaineering tent, and the lightweight options are truly astonishing. You can get a solid, large, freestanding tent for three pounds, or you can go down to even two pounds with a trekking pole tent. Those who don't use a tent will often at least carry a tarp – something that weighs over a pound itself. So, carry an extra half pound for a full trekking pole tent. Freestanding tents give you versatility, so I will always carry one, even considering the extra pound. Again, weight is proportional to comfort. NEMO Equipment will always be my go-to brand for quality, lightweight tents.

Pack

When choosing a pack, make sure you put weight in it before purchasing. Packs will always sit differently on your shoulders and hips with thirty-five pounds inside, compared to when it's empty. The things to look for are a large hip belt and straps, durable buckles and a comfortable back panel that allows a good amount of airflow. A good pack will weigh at least two pounds, and usually hovers around three. Don't get a one-pound pack – it will fall apart, or be immensely uncomfortable with the necessary weight to survive for six months.

Sleeping bag and pad

In "real" life, your bedroom is a place to relax, gather yourself, and rest. When you're hiking a trail, that doesn't change. Where you sleep must be to your liking and satisfaction, or else you will become a grump. Sacrificing ounces on sleeping equipment (bag and pad) means sacrificing sleep. A down bag will always be the best option for tent dwellers. Lightweight and compressible, it's the best thing to use in dry conditions. If you choose to go the route sans tent, synthetic is a must. Down loses its insulation factor when wet, synthetic insulation does not. And since a synthetic bag retains its warmth when wet, when sleeping outside, or in a shelter, and a spray from rain comes down, you won't be you're freezing your butt off.

Regardless of what you use, storing it in a waterproof stuff sack is crucial. Prevent the unexpected from ruining your sleep!

As far as pads go – gets what's comfortable. For me, that's a three-inch inflatable full-length pad. Those three inches keep you off the ground, and create an even surface. When considering an inflatable pad, make sure you get something durable enough to withstand daily use for months on end. Be cautious of the too-good-to-be-true NeoAir; the material isn't the strongest.

Footwear

Now for the most important and hotly contested piece of gear – footwear. People hike the AT in everything from flip-flops to full grain leather trekking boots. You should go with what feels right to you. As long as it's supportive and comfortable, you'll be happy. I always use a full grain, full shank leather boot. I just feel more comfortable. Food for thought though – there are a lot of rocks, dirt, mud, and water. Something protective, stiff, and waterproof always helps and keeps your feet happier. Aftermarket insoles such as SuperFeet really do help to prevent any major joint problems.

The key things to mind in footwear are the sole and the heel. The sole is going to take all the beating, so get something with a thick tread that seems burly. With the heel, look for something that locks the heel of your foot in place. Movement equals blisters, so get something that will do its best to prevent any movement within the boot/shoe. It can take anywhere from one to four pairs of kicks. The more heavy duty they are, the longer they will last.

Clothes

You don't need a lot of clothes. At any given point in time, you should never be carrying more than two pounds of clothing. The fact is, you're going to stink, and you're going to get filthy— no amount of clothing will prevent that. The best system I've found is the three set system; warm weather, cold weather, and camp. Having a dedicated set of clothing for camp insures you will always go to bed warm and dry. Mental health is just as – if not more – vital to a successful thru-hike.

The more you hike, the more you'll find little ways to cut down on weight; items like zip-off pants reduce weight right off the bat. I get hot more often, so I pack lighter-weight, less warm clothes. Down jackets are going to be the lightest and most comfortable insulation piece, but make sure yours doesn't get wet. Once it' wet, it has little to no warmth value. That's where your waterproof stuff sacks will save the day!

When it comes to rainwear, once you accept the fact you will definitely get wet, you should save weight on the gear and get lighter, windproof, water-resistant layers[37]. This helps keep you warm, but saves weight by not having a Gore-Tex lining.

Three pairs of socks – two to rotate for hiking, one for camp – and two pairs of undies will be all you need. The best way to keep them from getting too nasty is to go merino. These days, brands have wool as soft as cotton; so don't be afraid to try it for fear of itchiness. Wool keeps stink down, regulates temperature well, and lasts between washes. Try to find socks with a little Spandex or Lycra in it, as this will insure they don't start to sag before you get to a town to wash them. Merino socks are, by far, the best out there. They will last for days without getting stiff, or smelling nearly as bad as synthetic socks, and they are comfortable. My two hiking pair of Icebreakers made it the entire Pacific Crest Trail – without any holes. Having a thicker, more cushioned pair for camp also gives you the added comfort at the end of a long day.

Stove

The biggest equipment debate after footwear is that of stoves. There are so many options: different weights, styles, colors, brands, versions and corresponding headaches associated with this invaluable item. From cat food cans to manually compressed bottles of gasoline-- if it's flammable, there's a stove for it. For an Appalachian trail thru-hiker, it is necessary to think about what it is you're realistically going to have access to, the conditions you will be in, and how you want to cook. I met people who were cooking solely over campfires; I left them way behind. Keep in mind, in the humidity of the East coast, making a fire is tough and time consuming. Think about working for eight to ten hours a

---

[37] Editor's note: Ian is easily the most knowledgeable gear mind I have ever talked to, however, I disagree with this *one* piece of advice. I went with a waterproof Patagonia jacket that worked wonders, *for me*. Ian is right, you will get wet, but a good waterproof jacket will restore to dryness faster than its water-resistant counterparts. Definitely test out different items in the rain for long periods of time to see what works best for you.

day, then coming home to spend half an hour collecting firewood, and *then* trying to build a fire -- not very motivating.

The best stove for me will always be a screw-on IsoButane stove. These will always be the lightest weight (averaging around 2 to 4 ounces) as well as the most reliable. Even in the cold temperatures during early hiking season, they work like a charm. Obviously, they make mountaineering stoves for a reason, and white gas is essential for certain circumstances, but not the AT. Take the simple route, have a couple extra ounces so you don't have to tinker with flammable liquid, and have the reliability of a true stove. Who wants to have an open container of extremely flammable liquid hanging out the side of their pack? It will ruin your day if you happen to spill your HEET (the gas usually used for cat food/soda can stoves) all over and accidentally light something important on fire.

Do it right, do it once. You'll be happy you can quickly and easily eat dinner every night. Primus and Snow Peak have been the most reliable and longest lasting fuels I've tested. The best thing? The AT towns know what you want and need, they will have plenty of IsoButane already in stock for you.

Food/Water

You'll quickly find what food system you can handle. Some people eat only bars, and some despise bars. You will eat a lot of peanut butter, Nutella, and ramen. Peanut Butter and Nutella (hazelnut butter with cocoa) have the highest calorie to weight ratio. There are about 2,800 calories in each one-pound jar of peanut butter, making it a great supplement to any meal. Nutella is a great change of pace when you start getting tired of PB – and you will.

For some odd reason, people don't get sick of ramen noodles. Ramen is essentially a blank canvas on which you can paint an awesome backcountry meal. One of my favorite recipes - two packets of ramen, a scoop of chunky peanut butter, raisins, and hot sauce; essentially the backpackers' Pad Thai. All the ingredients are cheap, you get some fruit from the raisins, carbs from the noodles, a boost of calories and protein from the PB, and best of all, it's good! I will add only one of the two seasoning packets though – otherwise it gets too salty.

Keep your conditions in mind when planning your rations for the next stretch of trail. If it's colder out, you can carry things like hard deli meats and cream cheese, if rain is forecasted, stay away from breads and crackers. Cheese will last pretty much through any weather and rarely goes bad.

Drinking purified water is a necessity when it comes to hiking the AT. However, you don't need heavy and expensive pumps. Chemical drops are the most lightweight and simple option you'll find. I only use bleach these days because it's so simple and easy to use: 3 drops per liter, shake, and let sit for half hour. It is always good to have a sieve or some sort of strainer to prevent any chunks getting into your water. So have one handy when filling water.

Luxury Items

This is the truly vital category of gear. No matter how lightweight and high-tech your gear is, if you're not happy, *you won't finish.* What brings you happiness will be different from what brings me happiness, but give yourself a few extra pounds to bring that silly thing you know you shouldn't carry. I carried a pillow on the AT, an iPad on the Pacific Crest Trail, and always have an extra large tent. I even tied a stuffed meerkat to my pack on the PCT. Mental stability is key to a successful thru-hike. You have to make yourself comfortable. If you are wet, cold, and unhappy every single day for months on end, you won't finish any trail. Break up the crappy times with a warm cozy set of camp clothes, an extra large tent and pad to sleep soundly on, and that item that just brings you comfort. The happier you can be, the easier it will be to finish a long-distance hike.

Planning gear is the fun part before a trail, so enjoy it. Use it as your entrance into the thru-hiker lifestyle, and take your time with it. On the flip side of that, don't give yourself too much time. You'll start to go mad with anticipation the longer you wait, and you also have a greater chance of creating some sort of excuse to not do it. Wait no longer than a year, and no less than three months. This gives you enough time to prepare appropriately and find what works for you, but not enough time to have thoughts of the trail consume your everyday life. Pick a date and stick to it.

Remember, you're reading this because you've taken on an epic task. Not many can say they have completed it. Research and respect your gear, find what works best for you, and stick with your plan. Everyone is different: don't attempt to thru-hike on someone else's gear choices. Take advice, but adjust it to what works best for you. With faith in your gear, you have one less thing to worry about. Plus, you will have extra energy to focus on reaching your goal and that will help you get there!

CHAPTER 12 LYME DISEASE ON THE APPALACHIAN TRAIL

I went into the Appalachian Trail with my share of premonitions. Most turned out to be false.

"Deliverance" gave me a bogus impression of the type of people I could expect to encounter in the south. The only people who told me that I had "purdy lips" were my friends, and this was before leaving for the trail. Apparently, implying rape to someone who was already anxious about his upcoming journey was their concept of a loving gesture. *Thanks guys.* As it turns out, people from the south are nothing other than exceptionally friendly.

The image of a black bear wanting to claw my face off also proved incorrect. Although there *are* bears to be afraid of (grizzly, polar, Chicago), the black bears around the AT are essentially giant raccoons. Their sole purpose is to dig through trash. It's really quite amusing to watch a three hundred pound animal with supernatural strength and giant razor claws scamper up a tree because it sees a one hundred thirty pound female off in the distance.

My biggest fear going into the trail, however, turned out to be justified- deer ticks. More specifically, the disease these micro-bastards spread, Lyme disease.

About Lyme Disease

Lyme disease, caused by the bacterium *Borrelia burgdor-feri*, is the most common vector-borne disease in the United States and is transmitted through the bite of a deer tick. Symptoms include fever, headache, stiff joints, fatigue, depression and the common "bulls-eye" rash. If left untreated, symptoms can increase in severity including permanent damage to joints, heart, and central nervous system, and eventually death.

Here's why Lyme disease is a big risk to Appalachian Trail thru-hikers- these early stage symptoms, minus depression, are also common symptoms of long distance backpacking. If hikers assumed they had Lyme disease every time they experienced stiff joints or fatigue, they would become hypochondriacs. Even the common bulls-eye rash, as it turns out, isn't foolproof. An infected tick bite can result in a variety of different rash patterns, including no rash at all. In other words, the only symptom of Lyme disease that deviates from the normal side effects of backpacking isn't even all that reliable.

Deer ticks can range in size from a fleck of black pepper, in the nymph stage, to roughly half the circumference of a dime as an adult. If removed quickly (usually less than twenty four to forty eight hours), there is little risk of the bacteria being transmitted into your bloodstream. Finding a brownish half-dime on your skin shouldn't be all that challenging.

Here's the problem- people are far more likely to contract the disease from the nymphs[38]. That's right, the fleck of black pepper is the more dangerous of the two. Scanning your *nether regions* for a fleck of black pepper after a grueling day of backpacking through the mountains is about as fun as paying taxes.

During my five months on trail, I heard of at least eight cases of people getting off the trail due to Lyme

---

[38]   *Deer   tick   ecology.*   Retrieved   from
http://www.aldf.com/deerTickEcology.shtml

Disease. Two people who I spent a significant time hiking with, *Road Dog* and *Wildcat,* didn't find out that they contracted the disease until after getting off the trail (one is now symptom free, while the other is still battling nerve damage, headaches, and blurred vision). I can only imagine how many hikers receive this bad news upon returning home.

The Data

In 2009, there were 29,959 reported cases of Lyme disease[39]. This number is projected to be as high as 420,00 when including the estimated unreported cases[40]. This is up 69% from 2000, less than ten years prior. And 2012 is projected to be "the worst year for Lyme disease risk ever."[41]

All it takes is a quick Google search of "map Lyme disease" to see that Virginia, West Virginia, Maryland, Pennsylvania, New York, and New England mark the region with the greatest prominence of this disease. In other words, the latter half of the Appalachian Trail possesses the country's greatest risk of this potentially debilitating disease.

The purpose of this chapter is not to dissuade you from hiking the Appalachian Trail. Even with this risk, the AT is a joyous and life-altering journey. But it is important for you to be cognizant of the risks and prepare yourself accordingly. Ignorance is not bliss. *Ignorance is Lyme disease.*

---

[39] *Reported Lyme Disease Cases by State.* Retrieved from
http://www.cdc.gov/lyme/stats/chartstables/reportedcases_statelocalit y.html
[40] *Under Our Skin.* Dir. Andy Abrahams Wilson. Open Eye Pictures. 2008. Film.
[41] *After Lean Acorn Crop in Northeast, Even People May Feel The Effects.* Retrieved from
http://www.nytimes.com/2011/12/03/nyregion/boom-and-bust-in-acorns-will-affect-many-creatures-including-humans.html?_r=2

Precautions

- **Get yourself some Permethrin**[42] Permethrin is a tick repellent spray for your clothes which stays active even after a few washes (and up to six weeks). Get a few bottles and have it sent to you every four to five weeks upon reaching the higher-risk deer-tick regions (mid-Virginia through Massachusetts). These containers are typically too big to carry, so spray your clothes and pass them onto fellow thru-hikers. You're doing them a big favor. Be sure to remind them of this when mom sends them cookies.
- **Wear pants and long-sleeves** This, again, is a "do as I say, *not as I did"* recommendation. I wore pants while hiking for a total of fourteen minutes in my five months on trail. I perspire professionally, so pants in the Pennsylvania summer would have made as much sense as shorts in Antarctica. Either way, it's up to you, but keep in mind that ticks can only suck what they can grab onto, and they're not going to grab onto pants soaked in Permethrin.
- **DEET** Sure DEET has been shown to cause neurotoxicity, kidney and liver problems, and birth defects, but damn is it good at keeping bugs away. *Of course, I am being facetious.* I used DEET a lot on the trail, and I can say that it does do a good job of making you less attractive to insects. It also does a good job of making you feel like *hot garbage*. The times where I applied multiple rounds of DEET in a day, or used it a few days in a row, I would always start to feel uneasy- slightly nauseous, prone to headaches, and occasionally dizzy. My DEET recommendation: use it sparingly. If you are going to follow the above advice

---

[42] I recommend Sawyer Premium Permethrin. You can go to zrdavis.com/permethrin to get a direct link to the product.

and wear pants/long-sleeves, apply DEET only on the days where you need a shorts/t-shirt reprieve.

- **Check yourself everyday** Because a tick has to be attached for thirty six hours before the bacteria starts to spread into your blood stream, the single greatest precaution you can take against contracting Lyme disease is to meticulously check yourself every day. I know I already alluded to this being a hassle. It is. But you know what's even more of a pain in the ass? *Permanent nerve damage.*

If you're not yet convinced of the severity of Lyme disease, I encourage you to watch the documentary *"Under Our Skin"*. This is a telling and disturbing account of the under-diagnosed and under-treated after effects of Lyme disease. Equip yourself with the knowledge to be safe.

CHAPTER 13 FAQ, ODDS AND ENDS

As a kid, I would always secretly look forward to the gifts that came in my stocking more than those that lay wrapped underneath the Christmas tree. Granted, the quality of the present wasn't nearly as good as the Nintendo 64 (still perhaps the pinnacle Xmas gift), but my anticipation for the smaller stocking gifts could not be touched. A Hershey's chocolate bar on one grab, a pack of basketball cards on the next, and topping it off with the latest Green Day compact disc[43].

This is the Christmas stocking chapter.

As I have said all along, the purpose of this book is to prepare you for the single most important factor for completing the Appalachian Trail- your mental approach. However, that alone though, does not fully prepare you for the trail. The focus of this chapter is to help provide some insight on other pressing topics. Through theGood-Badger.com, I have already received many, many questions from aspiring thru-hikers who are curious about all things thru-hiking. I figure if one person is willing to take the time to send in a question, there are a thousand others wondering the same thing.

Keep in mind that the following answers are mine and mine alone. Someone else may feel differently. But, by now, you have gotten to know my personality and style

---

[43] Back in my day, music came on a small plastic disc called a "CD".

well[44], so you can judge for yourself as to how well you'd relate to my conclusions. I will say this, it's impossible to know what is best for you until you get out on the trail and test things out. This FAQ section will help point you in the right direction and get you thinking about topics that you may not have not considered.

Questions:

How important is it to have a stove? What is the best stove option?

A stove is just shy of "essential." I'd guess that roughly ninety to ninety five percent of all thru-hikers carry a stove. At the end of a long day, especially on a cold evening, a warm meal is the fastest way to lift a weary hiker's spirits (after whiskey, that is). Nonetheless, for much of the trail, I was in that five to ten percent that did not carry a stove. I'm weird. I don't necessarily eat food for enjoyment as much as I do to satiate hunger, especially when tired.

You will probably want a stove. Dehydrated foods tend to weigh less compared to their dry food counter-parts, thus cancelling out (or at least reducing) the increased load of a stove.

In chapter 11, Ian went into depth as to the best stove options, and he is smarter than I am in this regard, so heed his advice. I will add that the JetBoil cooking system seemed to be the most commonly used on the trail. It boils water faster than you'd imagine, and is very fuel-efficient. It is somewhat heavier than other options, as well as more expensive compared to DIY stoves, but in my opinion, it's worth the additional cost.

Which guidebook is better, the A.T. Thru-Hiker's Companion or AWOL's The A.T. Guide?

Although I started off with the A.T. Thru-Hikers' Companion it didn't take long before I traded it in for AWOL's The A.T. Guide. AWOL's Guide not only differentiates itself by

---

44 Sorry about that.

providing an elevation profile (which allows you to more accurately predict your hiking pace), but also offers much more water-source and campsite locations without compromising on the depth of in-town information[45]. Although I am a proponent of supporting the Appalachian Trail Conservancy whenever possible, as of 2011, their guide is second-rate compared to AWOL's Guide. You can show your support for the great workers and volunteers that make up the conservancy by getting an ATC membership.

What did you find to be the best nutritional system for you?

I played around with this a lot as I was under the assumption that my fatigue was somehow related to an inadequate diet. As you already know, poor eating habits ultimately didn't cause my low energy, *an asshole mosquito did.* Nonetheless, there was a clear difference in my energy level with different dietary patterns.

Prior to a big climb, for quick bursts of energy, I would focus on simple carbohydrates: cookies, bread, chocolate bars, candy, Gatorade and so on. Although this does little to keep you satiated for an extended period of time, your body quickly turns the sugar (glucose) into energy. If your glucose stores are drained prior to a big climb, there is an increased sense of fatigue during the increased workload.

For more moderate ascents and descents throughout a typical day, I would focus on combining carbohydrates with fat and/or protein to slow down the rate of digestion and keep my blood sugar levels more stable. An example of this would be a tortilla filled with a couple tablespoons of peanut or almond butter, honey, and a banana. Add some trail mix for bonus taste points.

I was also quite conscious of trying not to lose too much muscle mass on the trail. The best way to prevent muscle loss is through increased protein intake. Because

---

[45] Includes information on lodging, restaurants, outfitters, grocery stores, libraries, shuttle services and so on.

protein tends to be more expensive and there are only a limited amount of options to get it on the trail (jerky, summer sausage, tuna & chicken packets), I added whey protein into my daily diet. This helped to prevent muscle atrophy and keep me more satiated throughout the day as it prevented large swings in blood sugar levels.

Dinners tended to favor fat and protein more than anything else, as I wanted to repair damaged muscle tissue while resting. Plus, this helped to avoid waking up with a drastically lowered blood sugar level in the morning (the trigger for hunger). Typical dinners included a large tuna packet and cheddar cheese inside of a tortilla (the ultimate trail food – go whole wheat for bonus fiber points), with a candy bar and protein drink for dessert.

However, everyone's body will react differently on the trail. Some people consumed upwards of 8,000 calories in a day (an insane amount of food) and would be unable to keep any weight on their frame. Others would intake a more modest 2,000 – 2,500 calories per day, and still maintain a relatively healthy body weight.

Leap, a fellow 2011 NOBO hiker, was complaining about chronic fatigue halfway through Virginia. He was cutting his days far shorter than he was anticipating while taking extended naps during his lunch break. Another thruhiker pointed out that he wasn't eating enough throughout the day and that he needed to be consuming at least twice as much food compared to his current intake. Once *Leap* heeded this advice, his energy level and mood shot through the roof.

Play around not only with the amount of food you intake, but the variations of fat, protein, and carbohydrates and the time of day you consume them to see what works best for you.

What do you figure your actual costs were?

My actual costs were somewhere between $4,500-$5,000. I was less than frugal when in town. The wallet tends to loosen up after four to five days of deprivation and laborious activity. I could have easily spent more, but *you can easily get by for less.*

Some tips for saving a few bucks:

- **Eat before getting into town**. The fastest way to blow through cash is to go into town feeling famished. You'll order a milkshake, a meat lover's pizza, chili fries, and two Cokes (or Yuenglings) before you know it. A few spoonfuls of peanut butter in advance should help curb your hunger and prevent you from this frivolous spending.
- **Research which towns have grocery stores versus convenience stores or gas stations.** Resupplying at a gas station not only lacks anything with proper nutrition, it's the fastest way to overspend. Having said that, these are the areas where mail drops are most prevalent. Typically, if there's a convenience store, a post office is not far off. Otherwise, whenever possible, try to resupply with enough food to make it to the next town that offers a proper grocery store.
- **Buy your footwear from a company with a lenient replacement policy**. You will go through more than one pair of shoes/boots; it will more likely be three to five[46]. For this reason, getting your footwear from a company with a lenient replacement policy is *huge*. Salomon, Merrell and Keen have a good reputation in this regard. Be sure to mention that you're an Appalachian Trail thru-hiker on the phone. As Ian already mentioned, they like our kind. Before purchasing a particular boot/shoe call the company's customer service phone number and inquire specifically about their repair/replacement policy. Paying for one quality pair of boots is a lot cheaper than four shoddy pairs.
- **Become a member at REI.** For only twenty dollars, you become a lifetime member at REI. Go through them to get your larger gear purchases. Their return policy is the most lenient of *any* retailer[47] I have ever been to. You can pretty much return anything in any condition at anytime. I'm not suggesting you take

---

[46] Depending on quality of shoe. Another reason to opt for a reputable brand.

[47] Outdoor or otherwise.

advantage of their leniency, but let's call a spade a spade; you will undoubtedly buy gear that, for a variety of reasons, won't work out. When you get onto the trail and find out that your gaiters aren't necessary, that your fleece's zipper ripped off, or that the twelve inch Rambo knife is excessive, send it home and have someone return it for you or return it later yourself. Maybe you're planning on taking side trips into Washington D.C., Boston, or New York City? If so, all of these cities have REIs. If your clothes are beginning to wear down, exchange them for the new version.

- **Make your own gear**. As you might have guessed, this particular tip is beyond me, but I'm on the extreme end of the incompetent spectrum. I saw a lot of people on the trail with homemade gear, and not only was it cheaper, but it usually held up just as well, if not better. If you don't know how to make anything, find a friend who does and bribe them with alcohol or blackmail them with incriminating photos.

- **Ask hostels for work-for-stays**. Most hiker hostels are run by people with hearts of gold. If you tell them that you're strapped for cash but very eager to help in any way that you can, they will quite likely be happy to exchange your labor for a free night's stay.

- **Check hiker boxes before hitting up the grocery store**. Hiker boxes are usually at all hostels, outfitters, or any other establishment that claims that it's "hiker-friendly." Hikers leave behind what they no longer need or want. You'd be surprised what people get rid of. I've seen people do their entire resupply with hiker boxes. For karma's sake, don't let the hiker box be a one-way flow of goods, give back when you can, but if you can stomach shrimp flavored Ramen, hiker boxes will become your best friend.

- **Clean your clothes on warm, sunny days on the trail.** For me, the main reason for going into town was to do laundry. Three or four consecutive days on the trail renders your clothes smelling like the end of time. When in town, it becomes very difficult to not succumb to the sweet temptation that is ice cream, pizza, and beer. Instead, rinse your sweat soaked garments in the nearest moving water source. Be *very* conscious not to get soap near the water source. Either do a water-only rinse, or fill up your water bottle and take your camper's soap a couple hundred yards from the water source. From there, either fasten your clothes to the back of your pack and/or lay the goods out in the sun during your afternoon break(s). Not only will you save money on laundry, you'll cut back on the need to get to town, thus removing other temptations.

- **Start a blog!** One of the most surprising lessons I learned while thru-hiking the AT was how eager people were to help. This applies not only to friends and family, but total strangers as well. I received care packages, money, a blockbuster trail magic session[48], and a liquor store allowance[49], all from readers of my very simple[50] blog. People become invested in your journey and want to lend a helping hand any way they can. Even better than the Snickers and beer, are the new friendships you will form along the way. Be as transparent as possible, and you will attract an interested audience. Just remember, after receiving all this support, it is your duty to repay this hiker karmic debt when you can.

Is there anything you saw other hikers doing (carrying unnecessary items, wrong food/clothing) that you think would be important to warn potential hikers about?

The biggest issue is bringing too much stuff, and it's not even that big of an issue. Although most novices usually start off with fifty percent more supplies than they need, it doesn't take long to straighten that out.

The folks at Mountain Crossing at Neels Gap will give you one of their famous "shake downs." It's only three days out of Springer. Assuming you didn't bring so much stuff as

---

[48] The Dalton family rules!
[49] Seriously. Thanks again Tim and Jacob!
[50] And some may argue, stupid.

to break your back before then, you'll leave Neels Gap with a much lighter pack and a solid understanding of what "essentials" truly means. Be warned though, the people at Mountain Crossing have their self-interests in mind. They're an outfitter and will try to sell you their gear whenever possible. Use your best judgment and try not to let them up-sell you on unnecessary upgrades.

Otherwise, again, in the Chapter 11 Ian gave you excellent, concise recommendations for your gear needs. Use that as your guide and you won't fall into the "too much stuff" group.

I usually bring a big machete when I go camping. Do I need a big knife?

No. Although you'll be popular come campfire building time, it's both extraneous and way too heavy. That's a dangerous combination for any long distance backpacker. Even if it's only an extra half pound, that's a lot of weight when walking for *thousands* of miles. If you don't believe me now, you will once you get on the trail.

Surprisingly, the only thing you'll really need your knife for is to slice cheese, summer sausage, and open various packages. Take a few pictures of you posing with your Samurai sword before taking off so people can see how badass you are, and then leave it at home. You'll thank me later.

What did you do to protect your phone? How often do you get to recharge it?

Nothing. Be smart. On the trail, my iPhone acted as my mp3 player and camera. In the case of a camera, you need to be quick on the draw. Having some bulky protective covering will make that difficult. It was a risk to not have anything other than a flimsy case, but my phone made it through to the other end of the trail in good condition. Just be sure to protect it in the rain – a couple Ziploc bags will do.

If you plan on only using your phone when in town, again put it inside of a Ziploc bag or two. Ziplocs seem to work as well as their more expensive counterparts.

I recharged my iPhone when in town- approximately every three to five days. I brought a XTG-SOL1500 Solar Charger, which was more or less useless in terms of its solar charging technology. It did act as my spare battery since I was able to charge it through an outlet. Turn your phone off when you aren't using it and leave it in Airplane Mode when you are to maximize battery life. Also, the extreme heat and cold seem to drain the battery faster. It's more important to turn it off in these conditions.

How can I obtain sponsorship?

That's simple- ask. The worst that can happen is that someone says, "No." In my circumstance, it helped that I already had a moderate following, which was the result of some Internet savvy, determination, diligence, and a unique writing style[51].

If you're serious about pursuing sponsorship, starting a blog should be your first step. Take whatever angle you want- make it gear focused, a personal diary or a series of comical posts- just be true to yourself. The more passionate and authentic you are- revealing your unique personality- the more you will draw people to your website. [52]

Once you've got a few posts under your belt, share your blog with friends, comment on other backpacking-related blogs, and find creative ways to get your followers involved with your site. People are excited about your trip. They'll be living vicariously through you. Take time to get to know them better. Encourage interaction. Give heartfelt responses. Be genuine.

---

[51] Write the same way you talk to your friends.

[52] Please, please, please, if you're going to start a blog, be true to your personality. If you say "bullshit" often in conversation, say "bullshit" in your blog. If you can write a 50,000 word dissertation on why down sleeping bags are superior to synthetic, let your nerd shine through. People are attracted to authentic. People can sniff out *bullshit (see what I did there)*. Opt for the former.

It's never too soon to start pursuing sponsors, but your chances of success will increase if you can clearly demonstrate that you already have an engaged community. Ask friends if they have contacts at any gear companies. If not, ask friends if they have friends who know anyone working for a gear company (this was my approach). Having a mutual contact will prove far more successful than making cold calls and sending e-mails to info@gearcompany.com.

People will be eager to help. You are doing something truly badass. Don't forget that.

If you're looking for more help, I'm building a full tutorial for those seriously pursuing gear sponsorships. More information on this can be found at: zrdavis.com/sponsorships

It is at this point that I would like to thank Hi-Tec (www.hi-tec.com), Eureka! (www.eurekatent.com), Tech4o (www.tech4o.com), Gregory Packs (www.gregorypacks.com), and Innate Gear (www.innate-gear.com) for donating quality gear to both *Badger* and *Whoop*.

How much weight can I expect to lose?

Most people lose a lot of weight. Toward the end of the trail, I had talked with people who had lost fifteen, twenty, thirty....even fifty pounds! That's awesome. Keep in mind, with very few exceptions, no one on the trail really eats a "healthful" diet. It's difficult to obtain healthful foods and they are more expensive, heavier and less calorie efficient (fruits and vegetables have a high weight per calorie ratio). Hiking the AT really is the only "eat whatever you want and lose weight" diet plan.

Nonetheless, there are exceptions to the weight loss rule. I lost two pounds. I talked to a few other people who lost very little weight, or no weight at all. It's usually because they have very little weight to lose. In my particular case, I have no idea why I lost only two pounds. I choose to blame the mosquito.

For the most part, expect to lose weight. A lot of it.

Do you feel that you ended the trail in the best shape of your life?

If by "shape," you mean cardio-vascular endurance, yes, and by a landslide. I've run a marathon before, and I wasn't even close to being in as good shape as I was toward the end of the trail.

Oftentimes people refer to "shape" meaning their physical appearance-where the only weight on their body is muscle. This is not the case. People lose weight, but they tend to lose it proportionately all over their body; muscle goes too. It's more of a Hollywood anorexia *shape* versus a Gerard Butler from *"300" shape*. This is true all over your body except for your legs. They will turn into boulders.

Why did you choose to walk from south to north?

I decided to NOBO because doing it any other way, in my opinion, is a disservice. I understand that some people can't get onto the trail until May or June. The traditional northbound hike isn't feasible for them. But crossing the finish line anywhere other than Mt. Katahdin seems anti-climatic to me. *Just my opinion.*

I crossed paths with others who were doing a flip flop thru-hike (starting at Springer, hiking north until a certain point, skipping ahead to Maine and hiking from Katahdin back to the same spot) and said that they got an intense rush of emotion going to the top of Katahdin even though it wasn't their final destination. It seemed like some regretted their decision to not go the traditional NOBO route.

But if a SOBO or flip-flop is the only possible way you can thru-hike, don't let the previous paragraphs dissuade you. Thru-hiking the AT in any direction is undoubtedly going to be an awesome, life-changing experience. If you're more of a loner, SOBO is probably the correct option for you. Also, like I said, thru-hiking about the journey, not the destination. You'll love the journey regardless.

My point is, all other things being equal, and you have the choice, choose NOBO.

(You can send angry e-mails to: theGooBadger@gmail.com.)

How did you deal with feeling disgusting all the time?

You may not believe me now, but you get used to going several days without a proper shower. During the first month or so, this is hard, and you might feel the need to stop in town more frequently than you will later in your journey. But I promise, you will eventually get used to it. This is coming from a guy who showered ten times a week before getting on the AT. The general theme of the Appalachian Trail is adaptation. Showering (or lack thereof) is no exception.

How many mail drops should I send?

This varies greatly from person to person based on his or her specific needs. You can very realistically get away with zero mail drops. I know this goes against conventional wisdom, but you'll have access to food in every town. Get small toiletry items when you have access to a Wal-Mart, and the various odds and ends at outfitters when necessary.

If you have special dietary needs or take prescription medication, you will likely fall into the group that requires mail drops more often. When I was battling dehydration (or so I thought) I had an electrolyte supplement sent to me every other week or so. During the first couple of months, I had five mail drops sent, and this was *only* because the supplies had already been purchased.

If you have the free time, homemade dehydrated food is cheaper and tastes better (assuming you know what you're doing). Go crazy and make dinners for yourself for the entire trip. But keep in mind, it's difficult to predict what food you'll be craving in a given period on the trail. You may make a half-year's worth of chili only to end up hating chili after three weeks.

Also, keep in mind that the AT is one of the few opportunities in life to live without any formal schedule. You do what you want, when you want. This might have been my favorite aspect of thru-hiking – total freedom. Trying to organize the locations and timing for each mail drop can be a giant hemorrhoid. *Again, that's just me,* maybe you feel different. *Hike your own hike.*

Another method- give trusted friends and family a certain amount of money before you leave for the trail, and e-mail or call in your requests a couple weeks in advance of your arriving at a post-office or other business that accepts hiker packages. This will allow more flexibility in terms of the items being sent compared to trying to predict what you'll want and/or need before departing for the trail.

How did you coordinate mail drops?

It's somewhat of a guessing game deciding what supplies you'll need/want a couple weeks in advance of when you'll receive them. Also, trying to determine where you will be in seven to ten business days is no easy task. Maybe you decide to get your package sent to the post office in Boiling Springs, PA, and you get there an hour after their office closes on Saturday. That means you're either waiting around for another day and a half to get $40 worth of Mountain House dinners and Snickers, or you'll need to call the post office and have it forwarded to the next address. Either way, the process can become cumbersome.

It is for this reason I would pick places a few days ahead of where I actually anticipated I would be, not only to make sure I didn't arrive ahead of the package, but so that I could adjust my pace to avoid the situation described above. Additionally, I tended to favor having packages sent to outfitters and hostels because they're usually open on weekends and have longer hours during the week. The one drawback of having your packages sent to venues other than post offices, is the verification process is a lot more informal. You run the risk of *anyone* picking up your package. I never had this happen to me personally, although I did see it happen to a friend. This is something to keep in mind if you're having something valuable sent.

What's a realistic number of miles to hike per day?

This varies from section-to-section, person-to-person, and even day-to-day.

As I stated in the Chapter 3, you should start slowly. Doing this not only gives your muscles a chance to acclimate, but more importantly, your ligaments and tendons.

Early on, I hiked between eight to fourteen miles. Eventually a sixteen-mile day was the norm, then eighteen and twenty miles. In Shenandoah National Park- through the southern half of Pennsylvania- twenty to *thirty* mile days were feasible, depending on energy level. Despite the headaches, I was moving a little bit faster than the average pace (I finished in 5 months, 1 day). Still, people were passing me throughout the trail. Some only had four months to hike the AT before needing to get back to school or a job. As I mentioned earlier in the book, Jennifer Pharr Davis hiked the trail in 46 days and 11 hours. Most people take around six months. Some people take seven months or longer. The people who push themselves past their limits are the ones who sustain injuries and ultimately fall off.

By the time you're a month to six weeks in, your body has adapted to the physical stress of walking up and down mountains all day with thirty pounds on your back. It is at this point (roughly) you can hike as far as your heart desires. Just don't let your enjoyment suffer as a byproduct of your pace.

Give chafing advice.

I am fully aware that this is not a question. Once we get past this technicality, this is quite possibly the most important "question" an aspiring thru-hiker can ask.

As I've previously stated, I sweat like it's my job. You can imagine how this was intensified while carrying thirty pounds on my back walking through the heat of the summer. Because of this, I suffered from chafing on a fairly regular basis. As a matter of survival, I was forced to play around with many chafing prevention and treatment products and techniques, including a hiking kilt. Seriously.

The most important advice I can offer is to focus on prevention. The salt build up from sweat is the cause for irritation, not the moisture. If it's an especially hot day, be sure to clean the *problem areas* as often as possible- maybe every couple of hours during the day. Rinse these regions with water (and optimally clean soap if you're feeling ambitious). This may be difficult and/or annoying to do if you're hiking with a group, but trust me, swallowing your pride is worth avoiding inner thigh fire.

Additionally, apply a body lubricant of your choice (I prefer Vaseline, others thought BodyGlide worked better), *before* chafing becomes an issue. In the beginning, I had a tendency to wait until chafing occurred before thinking to apply petroleum jelly. This was a mistake. In the summer months, apply even before leaving camp. It'll save you a lot of hassle later in the day. Reapply throughout the day, ideally after washing and drying the problematic areas.

Once chafing rears its horrible, ugly face, call it a day as soon as possible. If you try to push the extra six miles, you'll show up to camp looking like someone punched you in the face with a shovel. The discomfort will carry over into the next day, and so too will the shovel-in-face-syndrome. You're in this for the long haul; think with a long-term mentality. Once at camp, rinse with water, clean with soap (Dr. Bronner's or baby wipes), apply an anti-microbial (hydrogen peroxide[53]), and air-dry your danger zones over night if possible (in other words, opt for your tent instead of the shelter).

For me, the best form of prevention was proper attire. Over the course of hiking cross country, your underwear will start to lose its elasticity. When this happened to me, this was unknowingly the greatest cause for my irritation. Upon getting a new pair in Harper's Ferry, magically, I went the next few weeks chafe-free despite similar weather conditions and terrain. If your undergarments stop fitting tightly, get some that do as soon as possible.

My chafing became such an issue that I used a hiking kilt for a six-week stretch (this was before learning that my underwear were the cause). There are two benefits: one, improved airflow and correspondingly less sweating, and two, less friction. Both will lead to less chafing. The draw-

---

[53] Hydrogen peroxide naturally decomposes. If it seems to be losing its effectiveness, that's because it is. Toss your old bottle and buy a new one when you notice this happening.

backs include constant ridicule and trying to negotiate not flashing your R-rated parts when transitioning to and from a sitting to standing position.

I feel like that's an appropriate way to end this book.

Any more questions, comments, concerns, life philosophies, pictures of cats, or strategies for how we can achieve world peace? You know where to find me:

theGoodBadger@gmail.com

APPENDICES

The Dusty Camel Gear Checklist

- [ ] Tent (freestanding)
- [ ] Pack (Durable, between 2-3lbs)
- [ ] Sleeping bag (Down if using a tent, synthetic otherwise)
- [ ] Sleeping liner (Silk)
- [ ] Sleeping pad (Durable, full-length)
- [ ] Footwear (Quality brand with good replacement policy)
    - [ ] Insole (SuperFeet)
- [ ] Down jacket
- [ ] Socks (Three pairs)
    - [ ] Two pairs hiking (Medium weight merino wool)
    - [ ] One pair camp (Heavy weight merino wool)
- [ ] Camp underwear (One pair; wool, polyester, synthetic)
- [ ] Camp shirt (One shirt; Wool, polyester, synthetic)
- [ ] Camp pants (Leggings; Wool, polyester, synthetic)
- [ ] Hiking underwear (One pair; wool, polyester, synthetic)
- [ ] Hiking bottoms (One pair; wool, polyester)
- [ ] Gloves
- [ ] Hat (Light weight)
- [ ] Short sleeve shirt (Base-layer; polyester, synthetic)
- [ ] Long Sleeve shirt (Heavier synthetic material)
- [ ] Outer pants/shorts (Light weight synthetic)
- [ ] Shell Jacket (Water-proof or Water-resistant)
- [ ] Camp shoe (Comfortable, light-weight; Crocs common camp shoe)
- [ ] Stuff sacks x5 (Strong, waterproof)
- [ ] Cup/bowl/mug
- [ ] Spoon
- [ ] Water reservoir (2-3L; Playpus and CamelBak common bladders)
- [ ] Water bottle (Light weight)
- [ ] First aid kit
- [ ] Toiletries
- [ ] Stove

☐ Pot
☐ Guide book (AWOL's Guide)
☐ Water purification (Aquamira Chlorine Dioxide drops, Steripen)
☐ Head lamp (Lightweight)
☐ Luxury/comfort items (Pillow, mascot, journal, instrument, electronics, etc)

I am thru-hiking the Appalachian Trail because...

When I successfully thru-hike the Appalachian Trail I will...

If I give up on the Appalachian Trail I will...

ABOUT THE AUTHOR

Zach Davis is an Appalachian Trail thru-hiker, writer, and uncompromising dream chaser with a passionate disdain for convention. You can learn more of his latest voyages on his website www.theGoodBadger.com.

Find Zach on Twitter: @zrdavis

Ryan Mogan

Made in the USA
Middletown, DE
12 February 2021